T0327652

SENTIMENT INDICATORS

Renko, Price Break, Kagi, Point and Figure

SENTIMENT INDICATORS

Renko, Price Break, Kagi, Point and Figure

What They Are and How to Use Them to Trade

A BE C OFNAS

BLOOMBERG PRESS

An Imprint of

Copyright © 2010 by Abe Cofnas. All rights reserved.

Published by John Wiley & Sons, Inc., Hoboken, New Jersey.
Published simultaneously in Canada.

No part of this publication may be reproduced, stored in a retrieval system, or transmitted in any form or by any means, electronic, mechanical, photocopying, recording, scanning, or otherwise, except as permitted under Section 107 or 108 of the 1976 United States Copyright Act, without either the prior written permission of the Publisher, or authorization through payment of the appropriate per-copy fee to the Copyright Clearance Center, Inc., 222 Rosewood Drive, Danvers, MA 01923, (978) 750-8400, fax (978) 646-8600, or on the web at www.copyright.com. Requests to the Publisher for permission should be addressed to the Permissions Department, John Wiley & Sons, Inc., 111 River Street, Hoboken, NJ 07030, (201) 748-6011, fax (201) 748-6008, or online at www.wiley.com/go/permissions.

Limit of Liability/Disclaimer of Warranty: While the publisher and author have used their best efforts in preparing this book, they make no representations or warranties with respect to the accuracy or completeness of the contents of this book and specifically disclaim any implied warranties of merchantability or fitness for a particular purpose. No warranty may be created or extended by sales representatives or written sales materials. The advice and strategies contained herein may not be suitable for your situation. You should consult with a professional where appropriate. Neither the publisher nor author shall be liable for any loss of profit or any other commercial damages, including but not limited to special, incidental, consequential, or other damages.

For general information on our other products and services or for technical support, please contact our Customer Care Department within the United States at (800) 762-2974, outside the United States at (317) 572-3993 or fax (317) 572-4002.

Wiley also publishes its books in a variety of electronic formats. Some content that appears in print may not be available in electronic books. For more information about Wiley products, visit our web site at www.wiley.com.

Library of Congress Cataloging-in-Publication Data:

Cofnas, Abe.
 Sentiment indicators: Renko, price break, Kagi, point and figure : what they are and how to use them to trade / Abe Cofnas. – 1st ed.
  p. cm.
 Includes bibliographical references and index.
 Summary: "A noted charting expert shows how to use Renko, price break, Kagi, and related sentiment indicators in any market. This book introduces these little-known technical analysis tools to active traders, and is filled with key information on how to use them"–Provided by publisher.
  ISBN 978-1-57660-347-5 (alk. paper)
 1. Stocks–Charts, diagrams, etc. 2. Technical analysis (Investment analysis) I. Title.

 HG4638.C64 2010
 332.63'2042–dc22   2010002402

10 9 8 7 6 5 4 3 2 1

This book builds upon the knowledge gained from working with my students all over the world. Through them, I gained a deeper understanding of the role of emotions in markets and analysis.

A special note is due to my wife, Paula, whose support during the research and writing of this book was indispensable.

Contents

Acknowledgments

I want to acknowledge the assistance of Professor Hadley Wickham at Rice University and Joe Egbulefu, PhD candidate in the Department of Statistics, Rice University who provide invaluable assistance in R-graphics programs, and Sridhar Iyer, PhD who provided valuable assistance in formulating the architecture of the Price Landmark Matrix. I also want to express my gratitude to my wife Paula for her support during the process of creating this book.

Introduction

THE PURPOSE OF this book is to give beginning and more experienced traders a fresh look at the principles and applications of alternative charting types. These charts share one significant attribute: they display information independent of time. These types include price break; Kagi; Renko; point and figure, and cycle charts. These charts are important because when the trader applies them correctly, they provide different views of the shape of market sentiment as well as the shape of trends. The hoped-for result is that they will give the trader an enhanced ability to detect changes in price action. The use of these charts can have a significant impact on trader fitness levels, which most traders are looking to improve. (There are very few traders that cannot improve their performance.) There are even fewer that are consistent. A huge trader training industry supplies a seemingly unending stream of content and tutorials, in seminars and on the Web, with the goal of assisting traders. The search for new tools and techniques is all-consuming, but the ability to improve trading does not rest on a new technique. Rather, it centers on the trader's own behavior.

In over a decade of trader training, I have found that trader inconsistency and trading losses often arise from the central error of participating in counter-trend trading, as well as timing errors. While there are many other sources of strategic and tactical trading errors, this book focuses on the critical area of measuring sentiment changes. When all is said and done about trading, all prices reflect sentiment. Being able to visualize sentiment more accurately can have a huge impact on the trader's ability to achieve a professional level of fitness. To use an

1

evolutionary metaphor, if traders were a species, to survive they would need to replicate successful trades, select entries and exits, and adapt new strategies to changing markets. These are all skills essential to evolving into an accomplished trader.

This book evaluates and applies price break charts, Kagi charts, Renko charts, and point and figure charts because they all provide alternative and often superior visualizations of price action. They convey an enhanced ability to measure sentiment. These alternative charts all have something else in common: they originated before the computer. Additionally, they commonly remove time as an input variable. As a result, the patterns and forms they generate act as "landmarks" and "maps" of market sentiment. Our goals are to uncover paths in these "maps" for trading strategies and tactics, and to show readers how to use these charts for their own trading.

The question arises: Why now? Why revive an understanding of chart types that have become obscure? Aren't candlesticks the accepted form and shape with which traders analyze markets? Don't candlestick patterns encode market emotion effectively? Do alternative chart types really improve projections and predictions? The short answer is that market sentiment contains within its concept many dimensions that candlesticks do not efficiently represent. When sentiment is represented only by a candlestick shape, or a cluster of candlestick patterns, the understanding of market conditions is arbitrarily confined to the shape of the candlestick. Candlesticks capture open, high, low, and close data, but they also include a great deal of "noise."

In response to candlestick noise, traders have used technical indicators to smooth out the price data and filter out the noise. Additionally, as global markets have become increasingly interconnected, extracting better understanding of market sentiment is more important than ever before. In the current globalized markets, the ability to compare different market information effectively can positively affect profits. Hence, the value-added potential of applying alternative charting to price data and also to the important area of consumer and business surveys is more important than ever before. Being able to detect a change in price action or project a key area of resistance or support not otherwise detected provides an edge to the trader. By using these alternative charts to project key landmarks, locations of resistance or support, or reversal points in the price action, the trader gains confidence in shaping trading strategies and tactics. The resulting directional decision and trade entry should improve. Price break charts, Kagi charts, Renko charts, and point and figure charts all provide different degrees of enhanced confirmation about the direction and strength of a trend. Used correctly, these charts will reduce traders' reliance on subjective opinion about trends and trend detection. Too much of technical analysis is not quantifiable or evidence based. We hope that the approaches in this book provide new ways to evaluate trends.

It is also our hope that this book will also promote research into new forms of constructing alternative charting with innovative features. There is great potential for embedding these charts with new features that will move us toward a "smart" chart era. Charts that track inter-market patterns, charts that detect cycle troughs and peaks, and even charts that track trader performance are on the horizon. This book is also written to stimulate new forms of technical analysis of sentiment. Charting analysis focuses on price action, without measuring the forces that move the prices. We know that words of key policy makers, central bankers, and experts influence the market. It is now possible to analyze word patterns directly, and we will show how current advances in programming can convert "words" into technical indicators of sentiment.

Ultimately, improving trading performance requires trading audits. Therefore, this book also adds a unique application to the use of price break charts, Kagi charts, point and figure charts, and Renko charts: *their use in performance analytics*. We show how traders can conduct and improve their own audits of their performance. They can gain unprecedented capability to detect trading weaknesses by comparing the path of their trades with what these charts showed about price action during that trading period.

The Decision Path of the Trader

Since this book is about improving trading strategies and tactics, a good place to begin is with a brief review of trading as a decision process. What we are referring to here is the path of choices taken by a trader leading from selection through entry, management, and exit of a trade. What we mean by *decision path* is the set of logical steps a trader follows in order to initiate a trade. First, the trader has to perform a scan of the market conditions. The decision process in trading any market should always include a top-down logic, which essentially means scanning the "big picture." This scan includes observations about forces that are moving the markets. It includes knowledge of economic and business conditions and cycles. The next trading decision challenge, therefore, becomes choosing the instrument you want to trade. This choice is very subjective. There is no single approach that points to what one should trade. Some traders may acquire an affinity for a particular instrument for a variety of reasons that go beyond pure analysis. For example, a trader who admires Japanese culture or is familiar with Japan may simply enjoy trading the yen. A person who works in the real estate industry may choose to trade the Philadelphia Housing Index because of familiarity with the housing industry. These factors are, as we said, very subjective. There is also a quantitative approach for arriving at a decision on what to trade. We can characterize this approach as the search for an interesting pattern. The search for an interesting pattern can be quick and almost as instantaneous as a blink, or can require a longer process of deduction.

In many ways, deciding what to trade depends on what is left over after one surveys the terrain to determine what is attractive. Finding interesting patterns is equivalent to finding "landmarks" in the price action. For some, an interesting pattern may be a peak or a valley in the prices. For others it may be the shape of a set of candles. Non-traditional charts can facilitate this process. Once selection of the trading instrument has occurred, determining entry and exit points are logical next steps. The resulting trade can be a win, a loss, or a break-even. At any period of time, the trader needs to be able to assess the total performance and identify strengths and weaknesses that occurred. This leads to setting new risk controls. All of these trading steps involve choices and decisions in a context of uncertainty (**Figure I.1**).

Ultimately, trading is about making choices under uncertainty and with limited information. In the current vernacular of advanced statistics, these kinds of decisions are "gray" decisions, in contrast to "white" decisions that have complete information. Trading is therefore also about costs versus benefits. All trading requires perhaps the most costly and scarce resource of all: time. Finding efficient tools that reduce time spent in analyzing the market *and* minimize losses is a worthy endeavor. The trader's constant effort followed is to reduce uncertainty. This challenge is enormous because the market is full of noise. Prediction is

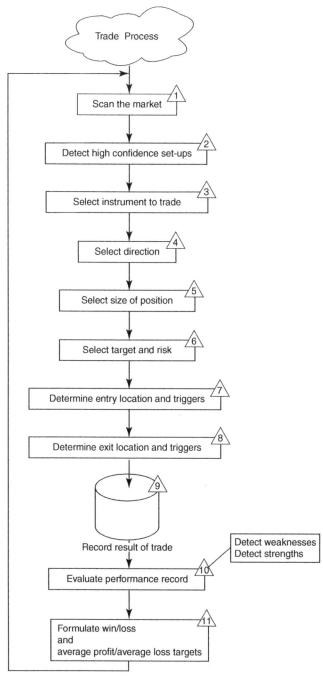

Figure I.1 The Trading Process
Source: Abe Cofnas and Sridhar Iyer

difficult and at best elusive. The trader tries to filter the noise and gain some information. All traders accept that price charting is the critical tool for navigating the market's chaotic terrain. It would be very helpful to think through the answers to these questions: What exactly are price charts? Do we really need them, and in what form? The answers may be surprising.

Price charts are a tool the trader uses to obtain an outline or contour of the price action. The raw price data is sampled from a price feed supplied by brokerage firms. The price data is usually represented as a line, bar, or candlestick. Depending on the type of chart used, the resulting visual outline of the price action will vary. Candlesticks are by far the most popular of the price charts. Line charts are effective when comparing one instrument with another. Candlestick and bar charts use the same sampling criteria, showing the open, high, low, and close. These forms of charting are by no means the only ones available. In this book, we consider price break charts, Renko charts, point and figure charts, Kagi charts, and cycle charts as tools that help the trader reduce uncertainty along the trading decision path. We will show that using these charts increases the detail (or *granularity*) of the price movement, enabling the trader to make a highly confident trade.

All of these alternative charting tools have in common two major features: (1) the elimination of time, and (2) scalability. A candlestick chart represents the price as a contour map of open, high, low, and close prices. These prices are sampled at a pre-determined time interval. A one-hour chart samples these four data points every hour, and a one-minute chart samples the data points every minute. In contrast to the candlestick method, alternative charting tools focus only on the price pattern itself, not its movement in time. Alternative charts provide an answer to these questions: Was a new high or low created? Did the price succeed in traversing a certain distance? Did the price reverse a certain distance? Time is not actually eliminated, it is an input variable, and we will see that it becomes an *exogenous* variable, or a filter.

The scalability made possible by alternative charting is also of great importance. What we mean by *scalability* is the presence in each time interval of similar patterns. Expressed in trading, the patterns at a short time interval such as one minute would be similar, except in scale, to the patterns at one hour, or one day, or one week. If patterns in trading are self-similar, it means that the concepts of support and resistance stay the same except for where they are located. A key feature of these charts is that we can apply them to very small time frames as easily as to very large time frames.

Using alternative charting clarifies the "fractal" nature of the market. Although these alternative charting tools originated before computerization, and (except for point and figure charts) were created and used nearly one hundred years ago by Japanese traders, their potential value is only now being tapped. With the advent of near-supercomputer power at the trader's desktop and multiple screen setups that are affordable, new levels of data presentation are now feasible. The result is a new era of visual trading in which traders are able to scan and survey multiple landmarks of price action. In using these additional charting types, the trader will be able to find zones of resistance and support lines that would not otherwise be detectable.

Each chart type discussed in this book can be used independently. As stand-alone charts, they increase the trader's ability to achieve the goal of detecting a high-probable profitable setup. For example, price break charts help project next reversal points better than other charts. Renko charts are very effective for detecting early and small changes in trading sentiment. Point and figure charts are particularly effective for providing a broad view of support and resistance lines. Kagi charts have significant utility for pinpointing points of change in sentiment. (See **Table I.1**.)

Table I.1 Best Uses of Alternative Charts

Type of Chart	Best Use in Trading
Price Break Chart	Detecting beginning of trend Projecting next reversal points Confirming cycle turning points
Renko Chart	Detecting micro changes in sentiment and momentum
Point and Figure Chart	Perceiving overall resistance and support lines Projecting breakout ranges Balancing bulls and bears
Kagi Charts	Timing of turnover of sentiment
Cycle Charts	Projection of future turning points

Source: Abe Cofnas

What would happen if we could integrate all of these charts and present their "signals" in a single table? The result would be simultaneous generation of multiple views of resistance and support lines, as well as alternate entry and exit locations. This method allows each chart type to generate confirming indicators for the trader. It is a premise of this book that the best way to use price break charts, Kagi charts, Renko charts, and point and figure charts is not as substitutes for candlesticks, but rather to use them in tandem with candlesticks and with a combination of technical indicators.

This book advocates using all five charting methods together to generate enhanced confirmations of key price points. We have developed and present new ways of organizing, quantifying, and interpreting the data to assist in analysis of price action from the perspective of these different charts. This is a departure from current practice, where analysts and traders focus on one type of chart at a time, with no interchart analysis. Consequently, discussions of alternative charts have mostly been limited to the analysis of trend, support, and resistance lines related to a particular chart. In the approach advocated here, price break charts, point and figure charts, Kagi charts, and Renko charts represent forms of data mining the price action. Each chart type provides a different statistical summary of the price data in order to generate a new shape on the chart. The premise of this book is that price break charts, Renko charts, Kagi charts, point and figure charts and cycle charts can, when used together, make a distinct contribution to analyzing price action and are worthy of traders' consideration.

CHAPTER 1

The Geometry of Emotions and Price Action

THE GOAL OF this chapter is to provide an overview of the role of emotions in price action and in analyzing the market. In this chapter, we elaborate on the relationship between emotional states and market conditions and identify the role charting plays in displaying that relationship.

A crowd-mind emerges when formation of a crowd causes fusion of individual minds into one collective mind. Members of the crowd lose their individuality. The deindividuation leads to derationalization: emotional, impulsive, and irrational behavior, self-catalytic activities, memory impairment, perceptual distortion, hyperresponsiveness, and distortion of traditional forms and structures.[1]

Let's make a key assumption that a price acts as a landmark. The question then becomes, "What is it a landmark of?" Of course, the visual path of a price shows distance over time, and as a result, the concepts and measures of momentum and volatility can be derived from that relationship itself. The structure of candlesticks and bar charts provide further landmarks. Open, high, low, and close, the four components of each chart, represent the failure and success of different emotional forces. The concept of bullish and bearish candles underscores the consensus that emotional forces provide the energy behind the price movement, and that charting ultimately reflects the emotional stage of investors, and consequently reflects the market itself. An entire library of candlestick charts and patterns has emerged that relates the emotion associated with a particular candlestick or pattern.

But we have yet to answer a key question: What is an emotion? This is the question William James asked in his article, "What Is an Emotion."[2] This question has yet to be answered definitively. Since James's time it has occupied enormous attention from neuroscientists, psychologists, and economists, as well as spawning the new field of behavioral finance.

It is an important question for traders because in many ways the market cannot be understood without reference to the role of emotions in price action. The market is in many ways a phenomenon of emotion. In fact, there are many metaphors that have been applied to the market: It is a great ocean, a battlefield. Traders have been referred to as "gladiators" and "surfers." All of these metaphors try to capture an aspect of a market that is perhaps one of the most complex entities ever evolved by human behavior.

Perhaps the most useful approach that has arisen is the characterization of price movement as signatures of fear and greed. In reality, these terms are generic categories that try to capture variations in the emotions involved. *Market sentiment, risk appetite*, and *risk aversion* are among the most frequent terms used to unpack the meaning of emotions. We are all familiar with characterizations, such as "the market was surprised," that speak of the market as if it was an emotionally intelligent entity. Perhaps this assumption is not far from the truth.

The challenge, however, is to give greater shape to what we mean by market sentiment. How do we quantify it? Let's start by clarifying what we mean by *emotions* and *sentiment*, and define some key terms, before we explore how the market patterns express them. In itself, the language associated with emotions demonstrates that the subject is not simple. Words such as *feelings, desires, sentiments*, and *mood* are commonly used to refer to emotions. The concept of the market as an emotional machine, or an entity that processes emotions, is a very useful way of thinking about the market. When a price changes, it is the result of the dominance of one emotion over another. The tug of war between "bulls" and "bears" reflects the concept of an ever-present emotional conflict in the market. But market prices represent a result of millions of individual emotional decisions. Each individual decision is influenced by a set of investment emotions and other decisions. The patterns in the charts emerge as group emotional expressions that express the "mood" of the market.

We still need to answer the question, what are emotions? At least, we need to try to answer it from an investor and trader perspective. Emotions are always about something. When an individual has an emotion, it has to relate to an "object" of emotion. Traders become excited about an earnings report or fearful of an economic downturn. The investor, trader, or money manager operates on that emotion and makes a trading decision. The motivation behind the decision is a complex web of influences that cannot be clearly deciphered. Market and sector indexes become composites of the emotional decisions of investors and institutional opinions. Prices, therefore, become mass behavioral signatures.

When a market reacts to "statements" of policy leaders or central bankers, the market is in effect an emotional being reacting to the words! That is why words move markets. As a result, the science of text mining is becoming a serious trading tool. This phenomenon is often called *herding* or *crowd behavior.* The presence of crowd behavior is now being recognized as a critical factor contributing to market crashes. Simply put, a market crash is an extreme emotional event associated with a high degree of the same emotion being mimicked. In crashes, the emotional contagion is that of uncertainty, and therefore a breakdown happens in the usual balance of sentiment between bullish investors and bearish investors. In bubbles, the emotional contagion is that of euphoria, or greed. Both represent an imbalance between the sentiments of pessimism and optimism. The precursors to crashes and bubbles can be detected in the charts as they change shape in response to changes in the mix of emotions that dominate the market. We all intuitively have experienced "the calm before the storm": high emotional states that accompany increased volatility. There is no doubt that the market speaks the language of emotions.

Where does all this complexity leave the average trader who wants to gain an edge? The answer is that any serious student of the markets or trader must gain a deeper understanding of how the role of charting provides not only a visual path for price movement, but also an emotional map. Every chart can play a role in helping the trader detect and visualize the emotional processes or stages that the market is displaying. Elaborating on the concept that an emotion must be "about something" to be meaningful, let's list the key emotions that are involved in price movements and link them to a shape. There are nuances, of course, in looking at price as a visual path for expressing emotions. A key nuance is *temperament*. Each emotion has degrees of temperament. Measuring temperament is challenging. Multiple–time-frame analysis is one way of doing so, where by comparing charts on different time intervals, such as four hours, fifteen minutes, five minutes, one minute, or ticks, the shape and stability of the emotion can be better detected.

The set of emotions listed in **Table 1.1** is not meant to be complete, but rather to be suggestive of the key emotions that contribute to investor and trader expectations and behavior.

Table 1.1 Types of Emotions and Associated Market Patterns or Indicators

Emotion	Associated Indicator or Pattern
Fear of losses	Increase in momentum
Fear of missing profit opportunity	Early entry
Greed or excessive risk appetite	Parabolic price curve Breakaway gaps
Euphoria/exuberance	Sustained excessive momentum Sharp trend line (> 70 degrees)
Shame	Crowd behavior
Surprise	Spikes
Anticipation	Spikes
Disappointment	Retracement
Exhaustion	Retracement failure
Anxiety	Sideways channel
Doji	Multiple probes of resistance/support
Confidence	Trend channel Trend line greater than 45 degrees
Accumulation	Retracement failure–Multiple tests of resistance and support
Regret	Retracement
Frustration	Multiple probes of resistance/support
Calm/equanimity	Flags
Decreasing certainty	Triangles/wedges

Building Investor Emotional Intelligence

If emotions are important in understanding price action, then emotional intelligence becomes a requirement of technical analysis. In other words, what does an investor or trader have to know to detect emotion in the market effectively, and how can one derive this knowledge?

There are several categories of investor emotional intelligence:

➤ Ability to detect emotion in market patterns
➤ Ability to detect transitions in the emotional state of the market
➤ Ability to understand what emotions convey about fundamental and technical relationships

A premise of this book is that an added benefit of alternative charting is that it gives an edge to the trader in detecting emotional phases in the market. When we view charts in this context, each chart type provides different abilities to extract or detect which emotion dominated the price action. The candlestick chart (**Figure 1.1**) provides a snapshot of bullish versus bearish sentiment. A white candle shows that the bullish sentiment prevailed, and a black candle showed that bearish emotions dominated. The line chart presents boundaries of resistance and support. Price action that comes close to the line, probes it, or breaks it reveals a state of change in the emotional stage of the market. Price break charts provide unique insight on the temperament of the market; because price breaks display only a break or reversal of a trend, they are key indicators of a shift in the emotional stage of the market. One may see point and figure charts, which generate columns of Xs and 0s, as measures of emotional continuity—almost as intergroup coherence emotions. Kagi charts pinpoint turning points when yin turns to yang, or vice versa. These turning points can be viewed as points of emotional turbulence or anxiety. In this context, we can look to various charting techniques as important tools, not only for improving trading performance, but also for building emotional intelligence.

We can now begin a detailed exploration of alternative charting types and their applications.

Figure 1.1 Emotional patterns and markets in the USDCHF currency during the 9/11 period

Source: Chart copyright www.ProRealTime.com

Chapter Notes

1. Andrew Adamatzky, *Dynamics of Crowd-Minds: Patterns of Irrationality in Emotions, Beliefs, and Actions,* Bristol, UK: University of the West of England.
2. Mind, 9, 188–225, 1884.

CHAPTER 2

Price Break Charts
Key Concepts

THE AIM OF Chapters 2–7 is to provide a basic understanding of price break charts, their construction, and their application in trading any market. The reader will learn strategies and tactics for trading with price break charting and analysis.

Pattern recognition is the science (and art) of inferring the nature of an object from the "pattern" of observations made on the object. Thus, given an observation, say a set of measurements from an object, one goal of pattern recognition is to categorize the object into one of several predefined categories. This basic idea is fundamental to much of science.[1]

One of the greater challenges in trading markets, even among more experienced traders, is determining when the pattern that the prices form provides a signal to enter a trade. This leads to a basic question: What is a price signal? *Essentially, a price signal is a change in the price pattern that alerts to a buying or selling opportunity.* A great deal of technical analysis literature focuses on describing what the ideal conditions would be for putting on the trade. A common phrase in trading, and a concomitant goal, is *achieving a high-probable trade.* An ongoing activity of the trader is becoming proficient at pattern recognition. The challenge is determining what kind of pattern is presenting itself to the trader. Is it stable? Are there underlying patterns that need to be detected?

For a trader to conclude that he has detected a high-probable setup, the trader needs, at a minimum, to have a confluence of all three of the following major factors:

➤ There is a clear trend direction.

➤ The price is at a key resistance or support line.

➤ The momentum has turned in the direction that the trader anticipates.

When these factors come together, they are considered to generate a high-probability trade. These factors apply in all markets. Traders use a wide combination of setups that include indicators to measure trend conditions, identify the strength of resistance and support lines, and detect volatility and momentum changes. Although we have not focused on these high-probable setup conditions in this book, in this chapter we will set forth a brief guide to what entry conditions would be considered high probable for a trade.

High-Probable Entry Conditions

The following checklist summarizes important criteria for identifying high-probable entry conditions. Of course, it is not exclusive, but the questions illustrate the need to integrate multiple methods of confirming trades while applying price break, Kagi, Renko, or point and figure charting. A useful exercise is to answer these questions whenever scanning and considering a trade opportunity.

A. Trend Conditions

1. Is the price above or below the day trend line in the intended direction of the trade?
2. Is the price above or below the fifty-day moving average?
3. Is the fifty-day moving average in agreement with the trend direction?
4. Is the twenty-one–day moving average crossed above or below the fifty-day moving average?

B. Reversal Conditions

1. Is the price at a day support or resistance?
2. Is the price at a four-hour support or resistance?
3. Is the price at a fifteen-minute support or resistance?
4. Is the price moving above or below a Bollinger band and then returning to its previous direction?
5. Is the price probing the Bollinger band and seeming to slide down on it, or hug it, if it is going up?
6. Do you spot a Doji candle at a support line or at a resistance line?
7. Is the price near a projected cycle turning point?

C. Fibonacci Retracement Lines

1. If price is at the key 61.8 percent Fibonacci retracement line, is it at a trend changing point?
2. Has the price penetrated the 61.8 percent Fibonacci retracement line?
3. Has the price penetrated the 61.8 percent Fibonacci retracement line and returned back?

D. Momentum Conditions

1. Has an inner trend line been generated?
2. Has the stochastic crossover occurred?

E. Risk Management Conditions for Entry

1. Is the stop loss less than 2 percent of the total cash in account?
2. Is the stop loss risk calibrated with the win/loss ratio?

This book focuses on a most important and particular challenge: detecting variations in the pattern called the "trend." Properly detecting trend conditions is integral to improving long-term trading results. It is well known that going against the trend is a major source of trading losses. If a trader became more effective in identifying and quantifying trend conditions, losses would be minimized as a result. We will learn that this can be done with price break charts.

Let's begin by looking at the commonly accepted technical definition and visualizations of a trend. The technical definition of an uptrend is the occurrence of higher highs and higher lows. The technical definition of a downtrend is the occurrence of lower highs and lower lows. Some technical analysts require two touches of a trend line to achieve the conditions of drawing the line, while others require three. The more touches, of course, the better the confirmation. The commonly accepted method is to draw the downtrend line by locating the highest high and next lower high, and then extending it out into future time (**Figure 2.1**). To draw the uptrend line (**Figure 2.2**), locate the lowest low and then the next higher low and extend the line further across the chart, following the arrow of time into the future. The idea is to obtain a sense of where the trend would continue if the price stayed within the boundary.

The classic use of trend lines does a good job of generating initial boundaries. Once a trend line is drawn, it becomes a contour map of where sentiment might change. Depending on the intentions of the trader, trend lines can serve as the boundaries of buying and selling

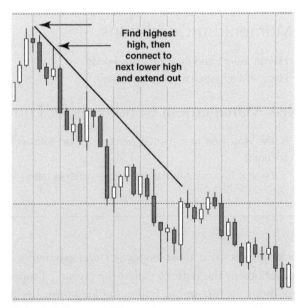

Figure 2.1 Downtrend Line

**Find lowest
low, then
next higher low,
and extend out**

Figure 2.2 Uptrend Line

zones. However, there is a lot of ambiguity for the trader who wants
to put on a trade in the direction of the trend. Several questions arise
in the mind of the trader. Is the trend getting tired? Is there a counter
trend cycle? Where is the best point of entry? How does the trader detect
when a trend is weakening or reversing? How does the trader detect when
a trend has been weakening? If a trend has been broken, when is that
break confirmed? This reminds us of the refrain, "The trend is your
friend—unless it is at an end." An even more important question is, "What
is the best set of price conditions for entering a trade?" This is an
ambitious set of questions, and many books exist on entry strategies.
Ask these questions of any number of traders and you will get a large
variety of answers.

The goal of this chapter is to bring the trader greater clarity in
(1) identifying and evaluating trend conditions, (2) determining how to
detect direction, and (3) diagnosing a change in sentiment. The result,
we hope, is that the trader will be able to shape and engage in trading
strategies and tactics more effectively.

To accomplish these objectives we turn first to price break charts.
Understanding price break charts provides traders with a powerful capability to be more precise about trend identification. As a result, their ability

to diagnose market sentiment can be greater than ever before. The rest of this chapter explores the underlying concepts of price break charts.

What are Price Break Charts? Basic Concepts

Price break charts have their origins with Japanese traders. There was little Western awareness of them until the publication of Steve Nison's book, *Beyond Candlesticks: New Japanese Charting Techniques Revealed* (Wiley, 1994). In effect, this book reintroduced price break charts to the United States. At this time, price break charts have a rather low level of awareness among traders. This is not because they are not effective; instead, it is because there is a common misconception that a charting tool that preceded the age of computers is not as effective as modern ones are. The current generation of traders matured in an age whose focus has been on fast execution, leaving charting as an afterthought. Once traders understand price break chart concepts and applications, they will likely apply them with a greater degree of frequency. Bloomberg Professional workstations have recently added price break charts. This will significantly increase professional analysts and traders' awareness of the value and use of price break charts. Let's look at the basic concepts.

Rules for Construction of Price Break Charts

Price break charts look like candlesticks without the wicks. They are bricks or columns. A good way to view them is as steps up or steps down in the direction that the sentiment is taking. They usually have a black color for a down move and a white color for an upward move.

The key condition that determines the generation of a black brick is whether a new low has been created. If a new low has been created, a new black column is added or "painted" onto the chart. If a new high has been reached, then a new white column appears. If no new low or high has been achieved, nothing is added. One of the most beneficial aspects of price break charts is the clarity of their rules. Because they operate on close prices, there is no room for dispute. But traders should not simply assume that price break charts are correct when they access them on retail platforms. One of the reasons this book presents detail on constructing these charts is to encourage traders who have programming skills to code their own charts.

Few traders have any idea of the construction logic that allows the conversion of price data into price break charts. The following logic statements clarify how it is done. For those readers who are programmers, these statements can become the basis for generating price break charts.

The construction logic has three components. The first element is the user settings. This allows for the settings to be a variable. Some programs restrict the degree of variability of the settings; traders need to watch out for this. Second, there is the base construction logic, which sets forth the key "if" and "then" paths. This base logic is followed by an iterative logic.

Here we present the construction logic for price break charts. It follows the rules set forth in *Beyond Candlesticks*. We also present a flowchart companion version of the construction logic to provide further illustration of the underlying structure.

Price Break Charts Construction Logic
Base Construction Logic

1. Read Base Date and Base Close Price.
2. Read Date, Close Price.
3. IF Close Price GREATER THAN Base Close Price THEN

   DPrice Raw upward white line; Uptrend Flag = True
   ELSE IF Close Price LESS THAN Base Close Price THEN
   DPrice Raw downward black line; Downtrend Flag = True
   ELSE Ignore Record
4. Set Previous High = maximum(Close, Base Close) and Previous Low = minimum(Close, Base Close)
Iterative Construction Logic:

1. Read Date and Close Price.
2. IF Uptrend AND Close Price GREATER THAN Previous High THEN

   Increment # Consecutive Highs
   IF # Consecutive Highs GREATER THAN OR EQUAL TO three THEN

Set Next Reversal Price and PreviousLow to the lowest price of last three consecutive white lines

DPrice Raw upward white line from PreviousHigh to Close Price

Set PreviousHigh = Close Price; Uptrend Flag = True
ELSE IF Uptrend AND Close Price BETWEEN (PreviousLow, PreviousHigh) THEN Ignore Record
ELSE IF Uptrend AND Close Price LESS THAN Previous Low THEN

DPrice Raw downward black line from Low Close of Previous High to Close Price

Set PreviousLow = Close Price; Downtrend Flag = True

ELSE IF Downtrend AND Close Price LESS THAN PreviousLow THEN

Increment # Consecutive Lows

IF # Consecutive Lows GREATER THAN OR EQUAL TO three THEN

Set Next Reversal Price and PreviousHigh to the highest price of last three consecutive black lines

DPrice Raw downward black line from PreviousLow to Close Price

Set PreviousLow = Close Price; Downtrend Flag = True
ELSE IF Downtrend AND Close Price BETWEEN(PreviousLow, PreviousHigh) THEN Ignore Record

ELSE IF Downtrend AND Close Price GREATER THAN Previous High THEN

DPrice Raw upward white line from High Close of Previous Low to Close Price

Set Previous High = Close Price; Uptrend Flag = True

Price break charts may seem simplistic because they result from a simple set of rules, but they unleash a great deal of technical analysis. From the perspective of sentiment analysis, by registering only the occurrences when a price is establishing a new high or a new low, the chart is in effect visualizing *the persistence of sentiment*. The price's ability to persist in setting new highs or new lows provides a way to quantify trends other than by using traditional trend analysis. It goes beyond the simple criteria of having higher highs and higher lows, or lower highs and lower lows. When we say a trend is in place, don't we mean that there is a persistence of sentiment? Viewing it from the perspective of persistence, the trader can begin to quantify how serious a trend is, when it is weakening, and when it has reversed.

Price break charts measure this persistence in an unambiguous way. Using price break charts, the trader cannot dispute the facts of the price action; either the price has succeeded in persisting higher or lower, or it has not. In addition, the trader knows in advance where a price break chart would be considered strong enough to break the trend. In the flowcharts in **Figures 2.3a** and **2.3b,** we present the computational logic for creating a price break chart.

Reversing Block Colors

A key aspect of price break charts is the rule for reversing colors and generating columns in a reverse direction. Using the "rule of three," a series of black columns will be followed by a white column if the high of the previous three black columns is broken by the new price (**Figure 2.4**). A black column is added if the low of the previous three white columns is broken (**Figure 2.5**).

Reversal Parameters

It is important to note that the setting of three is a default parameter and is not written in stone. The concept behind it is unknown. The "rule of three" seems to permeate technical analysis. For example, traders are familiar with using three tests of support or resistance as a threshold. In fact, the setting in price break charts does not always have to be three, and the trader should experiment with alternative settings. In this chapter, we will show that varying the break parameter by using up to six line-break settings can generate powerful new visualizations for the trader.

Selecting the Time Interval

Another key variable in the use of price break charts charting is the selection of a time interval. Depending on the objective of the trade, the

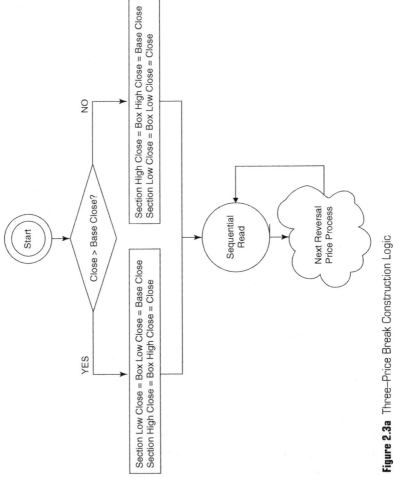

Figure 2.3a Three-Price Break Construction Logic
Source: Abe Cofnas and Sridhar Iyer

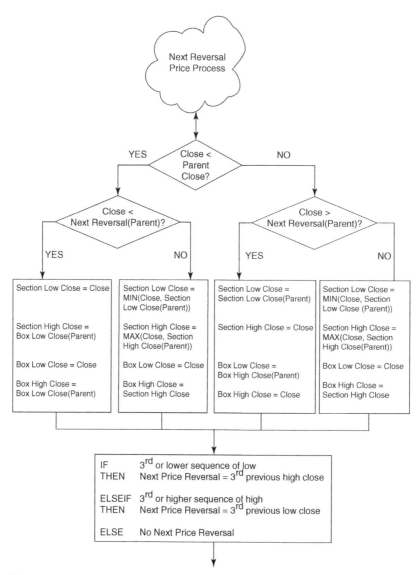

Figure 2.3b Three–Price Break Construction Logic, cont'd.

Source: Abe Cofnas and Sridhar Iyer

trader can choose from a continuum of intervals ranging from monthly break charts to minute–based and even tick-based break charts. Each time interval provides key information that can shape a trade. Combining multiple time intervals **(Figure 2.6)** with price break charts generates new levels of information that can support the trader in entering a position, as well as in managing that position.

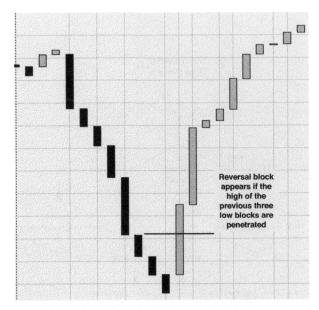

Figure 2.4 Conditions for a Bullish Reversal in Price Break Charts

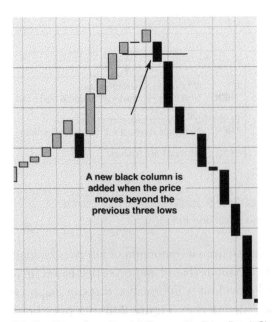

Figure 2.5 Conditions for a Bearish Reversal in Price Break Charts

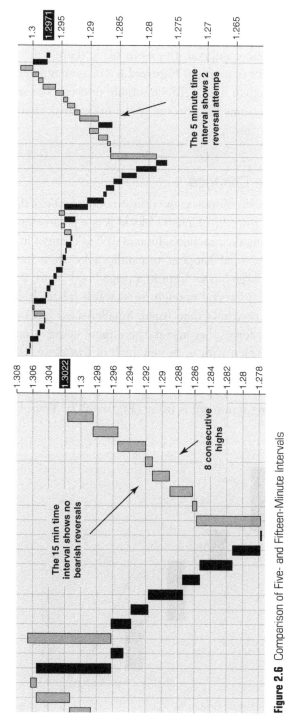

Figure 2.6 Comparison of Five- and Fifteen-Minute Intervals

Source: Chart copyright www.ProRealTime.com

27

The trader needs to be aware that there is a trade-off between the time interval selected and the smoothness of the price break charts. The shorter the time interval, the more likely there will be frequent price reversals. For example, in **Figure 2.6** a five-minute interval shows more choppiness than does a fifteen-minute interval. Too small a time interval will undermine the purpose of the price break charts, which is to smooth out the noise.

Column Shape Changes

How can price break columns convey the emotional tone of the markets? The shape of the price break chart's blocks is one parameter that assists traders in detecting the emotional tone as well as changes in sentiment. (This is similar to what happens to candlesticks when the body size changes.) When large blocks form in a price break chart, it means the forces have been powerful enough to establish relatively higher new highs or deeper new lows than usual. Smaller-sized blocks indicate a weakening of the forces, because the sentiment energy cannot sustain the distances traveled with each new high or low close. If the trader begins to see blocks emerging that look very flat, nearly approaching the appearance of lines, it is a sign that energy is running out and that the prevailing sentiment is tiring **(Figure 2.7)**. Thus, block shape

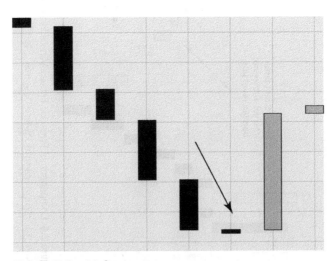

Figure 2.7 Bearish Sentiment

can be a leading indicator of an impending reversal. To the eye of an experienced trader, changes in the shape of the blocks provide insight into the changing pulse of the sentiment.

Pattern of Block Sequences

The presence of block sequences is a key visual clue. If there is a long series of blocks, the trend direction is strong but in fact can be entering an end phase. The trader's task is to evaluate when a long series is in fact in its end stage. There is no definitive, preset rule regarding how many consecutive blocks represent an entry into an overextended area. Block sequences will vary by instrument and by time interval. A good idea is for the trader to scan the sequences that have appeared over the previous week and determine how many consecutive blocks have actually appeared. This approach ensures that the sentiment of the immediate environment is captured, rather than a predefined view that eight or ten consecutive blocks represent a series that is about to end. If, for example, a trader using a five-minute price break chart determines that there have not been more than twenty-one consecutive black or white blocks, the trader can assume that if a series is in place that is approaching twenty-one blocks, there is a high probability that a reversal is about to occur. This kind of perusal of block sequences works very well. A more precise quantification is not difficult to achieve for the diligent, more mathematically inclined trader. In fact, one can generate a bell curve or standard deviation analysis of block sequences. It is also not an accident that Fibonacci resistance lines, when applied to price break chart blocks, often coincide with projected reversal points.

We need to state strongly that price break charts do not predict the coming of a reversal. They do tell us where such a reversal would be considered significant. Price break charts actually and precisely define and project *where*, not *when*, such a price reversal will appear. By definition, a reversal block will appear if the price gives back or retraces a given number of previous highs or lows! The trader knows in advance where a reversal will be powerful enough to generate a confirming new reversal color. We will show that advance projection of a reversal point can be a major tool in shaping trading strategy.

Flip-Flops

Upon looking at set of price break charts, the trader will notice that there are instances when a series of white blocks is followed by one

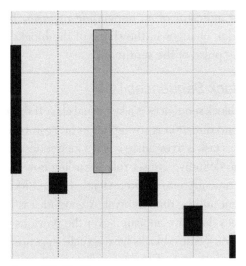

Figure 2.8 Flip-Flop

black reversal block, and then by a reversal to a series of white blocks. The opposite is also possible: a series of black blocks is followed by one white box, and then by an immediate reversal to black. This price action is called a "flip-flop" **(Figure 2.8)**.* It is a behavior that is very significant. It shows a strong failure to reverse the trend. An analogy would be a boxer throwing a strong left hook to knock out an opponent and failing to do so, thereby leaving an opening for a countering punch. The trader doesn't know in advance that a flip-flop will happen. Yet there is a strategy to trade a flip-flop. For example in going long, the basic approach is to put on a resting open buy stop order, above the latest black column, right above the most recent high. If a reversal down has occurred, the trader would place a resting sell stop order right below the previous close's low. In another example, a trader who sees a reversal down block would place the resting buy stop order at the previous high closed block. An aggressive strategy for a flip-flop would be to place more money on flip-flops than on other reversal patterns, because even when they occur it is very rare to have several consecutive flip-flops.

---

* Thanks to Reynolds Lee for this term of reference.

Reversal Distances: A Key Metric

When a price break chart reversal occurs, except for isolated instances of flip-flops, a new sequence of black or white boxes is set in motion. This happens, of course, because the countersentiment was usually strong enough to generate a reversal condition. Let's consider some important questions that arise in relationship to the reversal event:

➤ How strong is the reversal?
➤ Can the trader know?
➤ Does it matter?

These are important questions because if a trader knows how to derive some reliable answers, he will have the potential to generate very effective trading tactics.

In approaching an answer, it is useful to consider how we should evaluate what really occurs when a trend reverses. Using the example of a three–price break chart, a trend is considered to have reversed when the price has moved back three previous closed highs or three previous closed lows. This means that the sentiment has picked up energy and now is able to force a reversal. In other words, the price has driven through the previous thresholds. Therefore, it is likely to continue, because there is momentum behind it. New questions now arise: How far will it continue? What is the expected stopping distance?

We can derive the answers by counting the reversal sequences. It is unfortunate that platforms that offer price break charts do not offer analytics on price break patterns.

However, here is how to do your own reversal distance analysis for price break charts:

1. Generate the time series of the prices.
2. Locate the first reversal block (in either direction).
3. Measure the low and the high of that block.
4. Count the number of consecutive blocks (black or white) that appeared when a reversal occurred.
5. Repeat the process for every sequence of lows and highs.

To use price break charts effectively in a scalp-style trade, the trader should first determine the average stopping distance following a price reversal. Once he knows that average, the trader can shape several trading strategies based on the average. If it is almost always the case that a reversal occurrence results in a series of new highs or new lows, then trading that phenomenon with a scalping strategy is worthwhile to pursue. Each market traded has its own reversal signature, and in each case, data on reversal distances needs to be generated and evaluated. What are important are the maximum and the average reversal distances. Once the trader knows these two fields of data, he will have the ability to preset scalping entry and exit targets. We will show this in Chapter 8.

Consecutive High and Low Close Sequences

The parameter we call "sequence frequency" shows the frequency distribution of the number of sequential highs and the number of sequential lows that have been generated. This is quite important to the trader who is seeking to join a trend or put on a trade when the price break reverses into a new trend direction. For example, if the pattern over the past year has been that there never were more than nine consecutive high closes, it would make sense not to enter a position late into the sequence of new high closes. It would also make sense to use the maximum sequence registered as a target for a limit order. The distribution of sequences over time reveals the tenor of the market. The market has different phases. It can be choppy and reverse often, or can sustain a high number of consecutive highs or lows. A histogram of sequential high and low closes in price break charts would be a highly beneficial way of visualizing whether a pattern of consecutive highs or lows is dominant. Such analysis is unheard of in current platforms providing price break charts.

Let's briefly scan some price break charts along with their histograms.

Copper (HGN9 COMDTY) Price Break Sequences

The histogram in **Figure 2.9a** shows that down sequences of low closes only had one occurrence of six consecutive low closes. There were four occurrences of five consecutive low closes and three occurrences of three consecutive low closes. This market had one occurrence each of eight and nine consecutive low closes, and one occurrence of twelve consecutive low closes. The trading implication would be that by staying

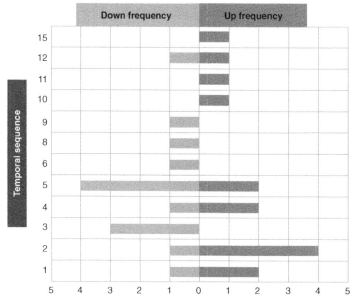

Figure 2.9a Histogram of Copper (HGN9 COMDTY): Start Date 7/30/07, End Date 5/12/09

Source: Abe Cofnas and Sridhar Iyer

in a downward direction on this instrument, a trader would be unlikely to reach more than five consecutive low closes, so taking profits after three closes would be rational.

The sequence distribution of high closes shows a skew to greater sequences. Copper showed an ability to incur fifteen consecutive high closes, demonstrating that powerful moves are embedded in this market. The up closes show that two consecutive high closes was the most frequent pattern. There also were three instances of only one reversal up. This indicates a choppy market.

Histogram of S&P 500 Price Break Sequences

A scan of the frequency distribution of high- and low-close sequences **(Figure 2.9b)** shows that the SPX is well balanced. Consecutive low closes and high closes were concentrated in series of two, three, and four. The low closes were able to reach a maximum of twelve in a row, while high closes reached a maximum of ten in a row.

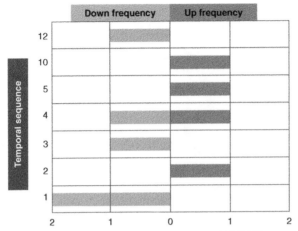

Figure 2.9b Histogram of SPX: Start Date 11/13/2008, End Date 5/12/2009

Source: Abe Cofnas and Sridhar Iyer

Dollar/Yen Up and Down Price Break Sequences

The distribution of high and low close sequences in **Figure 2.9c**, which shows a sample of dollar/yen (USDJPY) price moves, shows how difficult it would have been to have expected a long series of consecutive highs or lows in trading the yen. While this pair was able to complete a series of nine consecutive low closes, and seven consecutive high closes, the frequency distribution favored the lower sequences for both bulls and bears.

Gold Up and Down Price Break Sequences

The period illustrated in **Figure 2.9d** shows the strong nature of sentiment for bulls and bears in the gold market. When there is a run up or down, it can extend out. In downward sequences, the maximum hit twelve consecutive low closes. For upward sequences, the maximum was thirteen consecutive high closes. However, the bullish sentiment demonstrated an ability to sustain high closes of eight, nine, and ten in a row. This is in contrast to the sequences of low closes. Strategically, traders of gold in either direction should be looking to exit when a sequence is reaching its frequency distribution maximum.

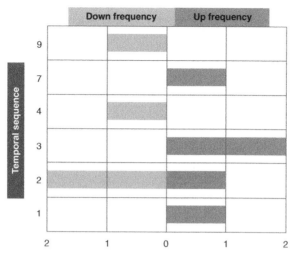

Figure 2.9c Histogram of USDJPY: Start Date 11/13/08, End Date 05/12/09
Source: Abe Cofnas and Sridhar Iyer

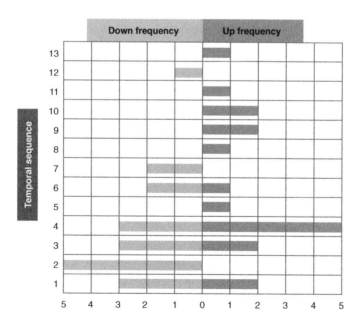

Figure 2.9d Histogram of Gold: Start Date 11/13/2006, End Date 5/12/2009
Source: Abe Cofnas and Sridhar Iyer

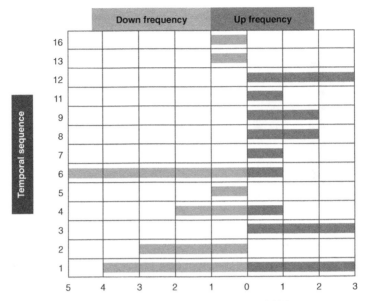

Figure 2.9e Histogram of EURUSD: Start Date 11/13/2006, End Date 5/12/2009

Source: Abe Cofnas and Sridhar Iyer

European Currency Up and Down Price Break Sequences

This sample of EURUSD price action (**Figure 2.9e**) demonstrates a great capacity for choppiness in its frequency distribution. It exhibited the ability to have four instances of only one consecutive low close—in other words, a flip-flop. Similarly, it has a frequency occurrence of three consecutive high closes of only one. The series of consecutive high closes showed an ability to have large sequences of six, seven, eight, nine, eleven, and twelve in a row. The bearish sentiment was not able to show an ability to persist to the same degree as the bullishness.

Is the Reversal Serious?

An important evaluation for the trader to make is whether a reversal is serious. If the reversal is simply a natural retracement, the trader may want to stay in the position and ride the reversal out. In order to assess the level of seriousness of the reversal, the trader can use Fibonacci resistance ratios by ascertaining the following information about the price action:

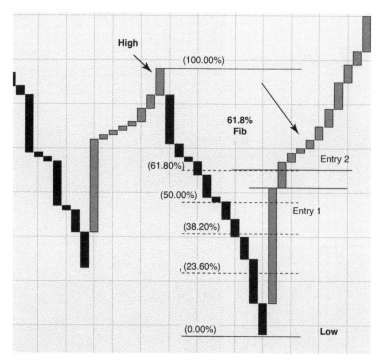

Figure 2.10 Price Reversal at 61.8% Fibonacci Resistance Line with Six Line Break Setting

Source: Chart copyright www.ProRealTime.com

➤ Is the reversal near a Fibonacci resistance line?
➤ Is the reversal in the direction of the larger trend?
➤ Is the reversal consistent with the existing ratio of the number of consecutive highs to lows?

The chart in **Figure 2.10** shows a scenario where the price reversed right at a 61.8 percent Fibonacci resistance line. This would be considered a good entry point. Notice that it is a picture of a six-line break.

Another important criterion for determining whether a price break reversal is serious is its relationship to the presence of peaks or troughs in cycles. This concept is examined a bit later in this book.

Chapter Note

1. David J. Marchette, *Random Graphs for Statistical Pattern Recognition.* Hoboken, NJ: Wiley, 2004, p. 11.

CHAPTER 3

General Trading Strategies for Applying Price Break Charts

STRATEGIES DEVELOPED FOR price break charts have in common a focus on entry conditions. Many of them apply directly in all markets.

Trading in the Direction of the Trend after a Counterreversal Block

This strategy entails the following five steps:

1. Select prevailing trend.
2. Select entry time interval.
3. Detect counterreversal.
4. Place a buy stop order or a sell stop order.
5. Identify an entry location.
6. Let's look at these steps in order.

Select Prevailing Trend

For traders who want to join the existing trend, a key step is confirming what the trend is. This popular strategy is greatly enhanced by the use of price break charts. When a trader uses price break charts, the strategy is redefined as *trading with the prevailing sentiment.* To find the prevailing sentiment, the trader simply needs to confirm what the latest sequence of blocks in price break charts is showing. The best way to determine the prevailing sentiment is to use three time frames. A big-picture time frame could include one-day, four-hour, and five-minute price break charts. A trader oriented to intraday trading would favor a set of thirty-, ten-, and three-minute price break charts. A scalper would use five-minute, three-minute, and one-minute price break charts. If there is doubt as to which sentiment is prevailing when looking at any time frame, simply zoom out to a slightly longer time interval. **Figure 3.1** shows an example of five-minute, three-minute, and one-minute time frames for three price break charts for the Dow Jones Cash Index. We can see that the patterns maintained their essential shape in the shift from the five-minute to the three-minute time frame. The one-minute interval, however, began to reveal some choppiness in the sentiment. The art of trading well includes knowing whether choppiness simply reflects the natural vibrations of the price action or is an important signal that sentiment change is surfacing.

Select Entry Time Interval

Price break charts do not change what time interval the trader uses to place the trade. Whatever candlestick chart is used for entering a trade should establish the time interval for the trade. However, because price break charts only record whether a new high or low has occurred, they take out a lot of the noise of candlesticks. Therefore, with price break charts, the shorter time frame will produce a more stable and robust analysis than the time frame used with candlesticks would. If a trader is using a day chart in candlesticks, a four-hour or two-hour chart in price break charts will provide a useful contrast and can be effective. If a trader uses a fifteen-minute candlestick chart, a five- or three-minute price break chart would correspond to it. There are conditions when a trader should use a different time frame for entry. This will depend upon the reversal distance occurring in the price action. By conducting a reversal distance analysis, the trader will be able to determine which price break chart interval provides the largest reversal distance. It would make sense to choose a time interval for the trade whose reversal distance matches the profit limit targets of the trader. Otherwise, a time frame that generates a large average reversal distance would give the trader a greater potential higher average per winning trade.

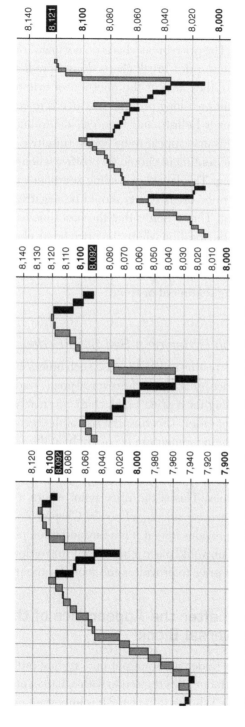

Figure 3.1 5-Minute, 3-Minute, and 1-Minute Time Frames for Three Price Break Charts

Source: Chart copyright www.ProRealTime.com

41

Detect Counterreversal in Place

Once the trader selects the intended direction, the key questions are when and where to enter. The price break charts do not answer the question of when to enter, because price break charts do not predict the timing of a reversal. However, they answer the question of 'where?' The trader who is looking to put on a long position first needs to confirm that the prevailing sentiment is bullish, and then can determine if a counter-move is in place. This may appear to be counterintuitive. If you want to buy into a trend, the sentiment should be positive when you put on the trade—right? Wrong. The larger prevailing sentiment is positive, but the price action in price break charts should be negative or counter to prevailing sentiment. The reason is that the best time to join a trend is when it resumes at the location where the price break chart projects the reversal. Thus, traders desire this situation because they can use price break charts to project exactly when there will be a reversal in the direction of the prevailing sentiment or trend!

Place a Buy Stop Order or a Sell Stop Order

Traders prefer these resting orders because such orders will be triggered exactly where the price break charts the reversal point. Traders often make the mistake of waiting for a price break chart reversal to occur before entering on a market order. This runs the risk of the reversal happening too late. The maximum momentum occurs right at the reversal trigger.

The trader looking to put on a buy position would identify the presence of a sequence of black or red[1] blocks in place, and then would locate the next reversal lines. This is the price point where a reversal block would occur. (The precise rule is defined in Chapter 2 as the reversal threshold of three previous lows if it is a buy and three previous highs if it is a sell.) The trader would place a buy or sell stop order that is slightly above or below that price to provide some room for the price to vibrate.

Join the Trend after the Appearance of the First or Second Reversal Block

In this strategy, the trader does not put on a resting order to enter the trade. Instead, the trader joins the action with a market order. The question, again, is timing. When is it too late? It is important not to rely solely on price break chart patterns as a strategy for timing entry of market orders. From a tactical point of view, though, entry upon the appearance of the first or second reversal block lets the trader join the action with a greater degree of confidence. Of course, a second or third new high or low may very well coincide with a decline in the sentiment. The trader needs to look at other confirming signals when timing market order entries. Nevertheless, once a trend starts, it is likely to continue in a sequence. In fact, the probability of the distance traveled on a reversal is quantifiable. (We discuss this reversal distance later on in this book.)

One strategy to assist the trader with timing entry is called *legging in*. Imagine a trader who puts on a trade on the second consecutive high or low, and adds to it on the third consecutive high. To minimize the risk of a whipsaw in the price action, the trader legging in would use a shorter time frame for the price break chart. The shorter time interval may be aggressive but it leads the action.

Fibonacci Resistance Confirmation

Price break charts work well with Fibonacci resistance line analysis. Both tools project boundaries that, if penetrated by the price, would signal an important sentiment event. A price break chart event signals a reversal of the prevailing sentiment, while a Fibonacci resistance lines resistance level break provides added insight into the significance of the sentiment change. Overlaying Fibonacci resistance lines will add to a trader's level of confidence when entering on a price break chart reversal. If the price break chart reversal is at or near a Fibonacci resistance line, this would generate additional confidence about entering at that position or increasing the number of lots placed at that position (**Figure 3.2**).

Entry Location
A price break will naturally first occur at the earlier time interval. To avoid false or premature breakouts, watch several price break charts simultaneously. A trader can decide to leg in first on the break of a lower time frame, and then add another position on the break of the preferred time interval. On the other hand, the trader can decide to wait until all three time frames have broken.

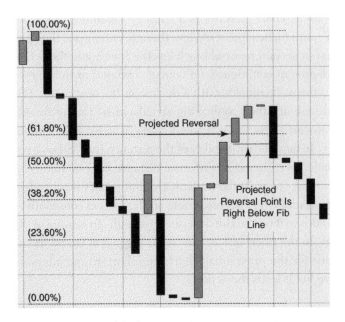

Figure 3.2 Fibonacci Levels and Price Breaks
Source: Chart copyright www.ProRealTime.com

Countertrend Scalper

This strategy is for the trader who tends to be contrarian and wants to join a countermove. When a trader uses price break charts, the following is a trading decision rule: the trader will put on the trade when the price reverses. By using resting orders, the trader always has a resting buy stop order or sell stop order on. This will ensure that the price is triggered by a price reversal. The key challenge is to decide which time interval is best to use for such a countertrend scalp. There is no predetermined best time frame, so the trader should experiment with several different markets.

The alternative tactic is a market order when the price has reversed and a reversal block has been painted onto the screen (**Figure 3.3**). It is a good idea to go to a shorter time frame for a market order because the reversal will occur earlier on a shorter time frame. This carries a risk that the reversal will be unstable, but gets the trader into the action.

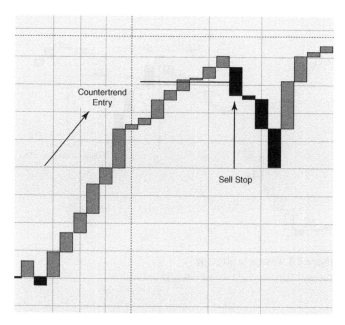

Figure 3.3 Countertrend Entry Triggers Sell Stop
Source: Chart copyright www.ProRealTime.com

Always-In Strategy

A key function of price break charts is to identify reversal points. A trader can build upon this function, using it to construct what can be called an *always-in strategy*. This can be accomplished by placing a series of open buy or open sell stop orders at projected reversal points in either direction (**Figure 3.4**). These positions would be triggered only if a reversal occurred.

Flip-Flop Reversal Entry

This strategy exploits the probability that when a flip-flop appears, any immediate reversal that occurs will be quite strong. To play this strategy, the trader will place a buy or sell stop order as soon as a reversal occurs that is counter to the trend (**Figure 3.5**). If a flip-flop occurs, the order will be triggered.

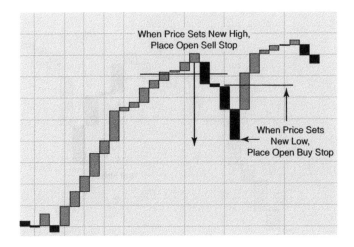

Figure 3.4 Always-In Strategy

Source: Chart copyright www.ProRealTime.com

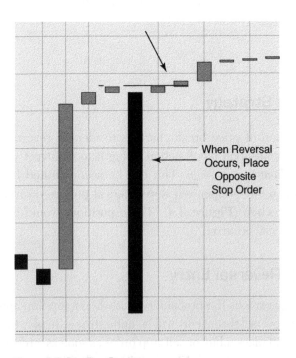

Figure 3.5 Flip-Flop Strategy

Source: Chart copyright www.ProRealTime.com

Momentum Trading—Six-Line Break

In many markets, economic data releases or sudden news events can cause a reaction in the market. The price action moves sharply, chaotically, in a spike and surge. Such movements pose seemingly insurmountable challenges to traders. A common practice among traders is to stand on the sidelines and let the market react to the news. However, price break charts provide a strategy for entering a trade in the context of high-momentum or volatile developments. By changing the parameters in price break charts to six lines and reducing the time interval to one minute or less, the momentum conditions acquire a shape that is difficult to see with traditional candlesticks.

Figure 3.6 is a six–line break GBPUSD chart with a one-minute time interval. Immediately notice the sequence of black bearish blocks. Remember that a reversal color requires the reversal to penetrate six previous lows or highs—a much higher threshold than the standard setting of three previous lows or highs. At the same time, the time interval

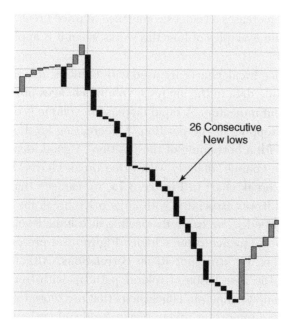

Figure 3.6 6-Line Break GBPUSD Chart, 1-Minute Interval (23/01/2009)

Source: Chart copyright www.ProRealTime.com

has been dropped to one minute. This combination contributes to a stable visualization of the action. Even at the one-minute time interval, one can detect a persistence of bearish sentiment. The chart shows twenty-six consecutive one-minute new lows! The most interesting aspect of the six-line break settings is that it allows the trader to detect stability and strength in the sentiment direction without the noise that usually accompanies one-minute candlestick charts.

Using a six-line break strategy, the trader could enter the position with a market order, even though the trend has started to resume. The idea is to ride the sentiment and stay in until either a limit or a stop-loss is reached.

Let's explore how to determine stop-losses with price break charts.

Price Break and Volume Data for Equity Charts

A commonly accepted sentiment indicator is the level and rate of change in volume. In equities, bonds, and futures, one can measure volume data. In spot currency markets, this data is absent because those markets are based on interbank transactions. Nevertheless, the presence of volume data increases a trader's confidence in price break projections. Let's see some examples of how this works when it is applied to price break charts.

When price break charts are used with equities, it is important to include volume data in the analysis. Volume changes provide important sentiment indicators. A rapid increase in volume is often associated with a topping of the position. A decreasing level of volume is associated with a bottoming of the position. A good idea, therefore, is to include volume analysis with price break charts. In the SPX three–price break chart in **Figure 3.7a**, we can see that when volume peaked it was associated with large price break movements. At the hard right edge, we can see a decline in volume levels and a flattening of the sequence of new highs. Figure 3.7a presents a visual analysis where we can spot likely correlations. Although further research on the correlation of volume patterns with trend reversals should be done to generate conclusions that are more exact, volume analysis has an important role to play in confirming the use of price break charts.

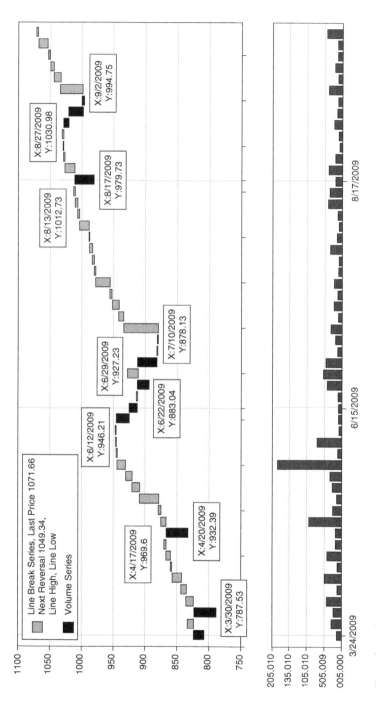

Figure 3.7a SPX 3-Line Price Break Chart

49

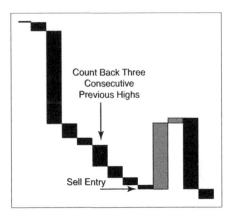

Figure 3.7b Calculating Stop Loss Positions in Price Break Charts

Stop-Losses, Trailing Stops, and Price Break Charts

Stop-losses using price break chart methodology involve locating where the price point would be for a reversal block to occur. The reasoning is that unless the price reverses enough to cause a new reversal column, the trader should stay in the position. Using three lines as the criterion for reversal, the procedure as seen in **Figure 3.7b** is as follows: Once a position is entered and triggered, the trader should, if selling, count back three previous high closes to locate the stop-loss order. If the trader were buying at the market, the location of the stop-loss would be back three previous low closes. This procedure for locating stops also works well as a strategy for trailing stops. Every time the price moves up or down a step, the procedure would be to move the stop along another block. It is important to remember that stop-loss tolerance should also reflect appropriate cash management concepts such as a maximum risk per trader or per day. If a stop-loss allows a potential loss that exceeds the risk limit permitted by the trading plan, the trade should not be taken.

Multiple Setting Intervals and Price Break Charts

An important question arises as to which setting a trader should use. Price break charts are commonly associated with three, because the setting is three on the reversal trigger. A better approach is to have several settings and identify which setting offers the greatest contemporaneous stability. In other words sometimes the patterns in the market will be more stable when you vary a setting. It may be more stable going to six breaks than staying at three breaks. One cannot know in advance, which is why it is a good idea to vary settings.

Here is an example of such variation. The best approach is to scan the settings from six lines, and then adjust the settings incrementally down to three until the smoothest pattern appears. Select the setting that has the smoothest pattern. The chart series in **Figures 3.8–3.11**

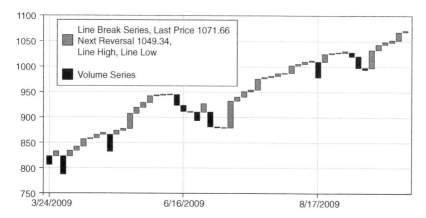

Figure 3.8 SPX 500 6-Month, Daily, 3-Line Break Setting
Source: Bloomberg

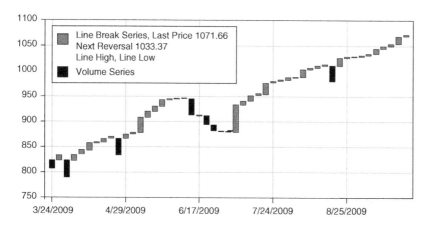

Figure 3.9 SPX 6-Month, Daily, 4-Line Break Setting
Source: Bloomberg

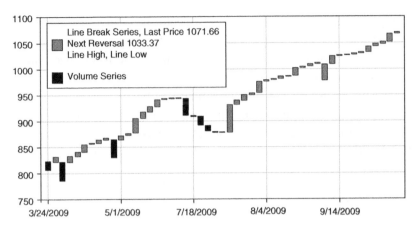

Figure 3.10 SPX 6-Month Daily 5–Line Break Setting
Source: Bloomberg

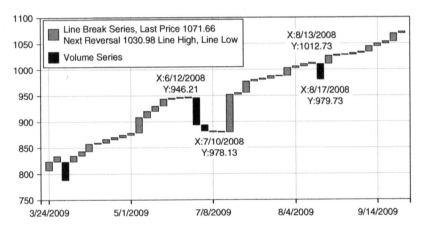

Figure 3.11 SPX 6-Month, Daily, 6–Line Break Setting
Source: Bloomberg

shows S&P Index data using three-, four-, five-, and six-line breaks. Notice how, as the setting increases from three lines, there begins to be an increase in the choppiness of the patterns.

Chapter Note

1.   In the illustrations to this text, red blocks show as black.

CHAPTER 4

Applying Price Break Charts to Markets and Data

THIS CHAPTER WILL demonstrate several market examples, using the general strategies we discussed in Chapter 3.

S&P 500: Price Break Chart Patterns Using the Day Chart

Price break charting of the S&P 500 provides a very good example of the applications of price break charts. Looking at **Figure 4.1**, we can easily see that the S&P experienced clear sequences of consecutive lows with reversals that were short in duration. After August 11, 2008, a reversal sequence started with six consecutive new daily lows. This was

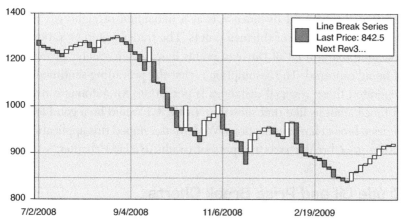

Figure 4.1 Three Line Break Chart of Daily S&P 500

Source: Bloomberg

followed by a counterreversal of one block. It flip-flopped and began a seven-consecutive-low sequence, followed by a counterreversal of four consecutive highs.

Let's stop here for a moment and consider some history. On November 4, 2008, a trader using technical analysis could have sensed that the prevailing sentiment was bearish. However, he could not have known when or if a reversal back to the downtrend would occur. He could, and did, know *where* it would occur. If the trader counted back three bullish blocks, he would have seen that the line low of the third block was 940.51 on October 28. Therefore, applying a strategy of "join the trend upon a break of low of the three previous white lines," the trader would have placed a sell stop at 940.00. The S&P proceeded to move down to 752.44.

With this strategy, a sell stop is placed every time the price break chart blocks are moving up. If the uptrend continues, the stop will not be hit, and if it is hit, the uptrend is likely to go enough of a distance for the trader to get a reasonable profit. The question that then arises is, "how far out should the limit have been set?"

The first method of setting a limit amount is to calculate the size of the first block that is reversed. The limit should be within the range of the first reversal block. This approach makes sense because the energy of the first reversal block is likely to be strong. In our example, it had enough sentiment change to reach the reversal barrier. The approach is also conservative because it assumes, as a worst-case scenario, that the reversal block is only one block long and is a flip-flop.

Let's apply this approach to the S&P example in Figure 4.1. We can see that the reversal distance was at a maximum of eighty-six points and had a minimum of thirteen points. The trader would be rational to conclude that a limit of thirteen points has a much greater probability of being captured. The assumption is that the prevailing sentiment that generated these reversal distances is persisting. An automatic reversal distance analysis like that shown in **Table 4.1** would be a good feature of price break chart applications. We have developed this application for future price break charts and present results in a later chapter.

Crude Oil and Price Break Charts

The crude oil chart in **Figure 4.2** is a good example of how price break charts provide an excellent way to project entry points. It is true that in

Table 4.1 Reversal Distance Analysis Sample

Reversal Block	Reversal Direction	Low	High	Total Reversal Range
7/25–7/28	Down	1234.37	1252.54	18
9/17–9/19	Up	1192.70	1255.08	63
9/19–9/29	Down	1106.39	1192.70	86
10/10–10/13	Up	909.92	1003.35	94
10/13–10/22	Down	896.78	909.92	13
10/27–10/28	Up	876.77	940.51	64
11/14–11/16	Down	904.88	968.75	64
11/20–11/25	Up	806.58	857.39	51
12/16–12/18	Down	885.28	909.70	24
12/23–1/2	Up	871.63	931.8	60

this case, determining the trend did not require price break charts for clarification. The price peaked on July 14, 2008 at 146.94. Let's assume that between July and September a trader still wanted to trade crude oil going long. Here's how the trader would have used price break charts: At any point, by looking at the price break charts, the trader would have counted back three blocks up and selected a buy stop order above the third previous high. On only two occasions, August 21 and September 22,

Figure 4.2 Three Line Break Crude Oil
Source: Bloomberg

was a reversal white block generated on the day chart. Price break charts would have kept the trader out of the way.

In the overall pattern, if the trader had chosen to enter on the side of the downtrend, the best locations for putting on a sell stop order were where a white reversal bar appeared. On August 21, a sell stop order would have been set right below 115.8, and on November 4, a sell stop order would have been set right below 69.92. Once the stop order was triggered, entering on the resumption of the downtrend would have enabled the trader to capture crude oil points with high reliability.

When the trend is so obvious and powerful, waiting for a reversal move to occur would not seem optimal. The natural predisposition of the trader would be to join the action. An alternative entry approach would be to enter a position in the direction of the price break blocks (the trend) with a market order, and then immediately count back three previous blocks to put on a stop position (**Figure 4.3**). This may result in locating the stop-loss outside of normal risk tolerance levels. However, it is appropriate because the probability of a reversal that is counter to the trend is much lower, especially at the first or second block following the previous reversal. If the trader wanted to reduce the distance of the stop from the open entry position, shifting to a lower time frame would have provided a shorter distance. For example, a trade

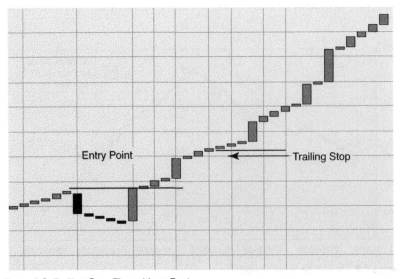

Figure 4.3 Trailing Stop Three Lines Back

entry on a one-day price break chart could use a four-hour price break chart to locate the stop position.

Do not hesitate to lower the time interval to the one-minute level, because it can provide patterns that are very tradable. The price break chart in **Figure 4.4** shows an example of using the one-minute crude chart with a six-line reversal, with a sequence of new highs and new lows extending forty cents. Depending on the trader's trading style, these intrahour trend reversals may be tradable.

Microdetection of Sentiment Reversals— The Use of Price Break Charts for Momentum Trading

In many markets, phenomena such as economic data releases, important speeches, and election results may cause a reaction in the market and a sharp and quick movement in prices. Such movements seem to pose insurmountable challenges for traders. A common practice among traders who anticipate an economic data release is to stand on the sidelines and let the market react to the news. However, the challenge for the trader—finding an entry position after the economic data release breaks—still remains. Price break charts provide a solution to entering a trade in the context of a high-momentum or volatile development.

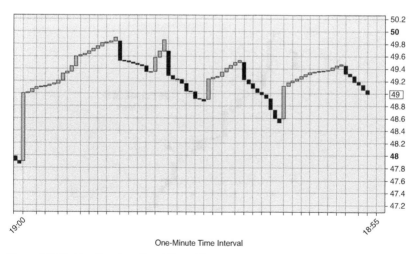

One-Minute Time Interval

Figure 4.4 Six Line Break on One Minute Chart

Source: Chart copyright www.ProRealTime.com

Momentum Trading: 6-Line Breaks and Tick-Level Data

By changing the parameters in price break charts to six lines and reducing the time interval to one minute or less, the momentum conditions acquire a shape that provides a new level of granularity for trading tactics.

Figure 4.5 is a six-line GBPUSD chart with a one-minute time interval. Notice the sequence of bearish black blocks. Remember that a reversal color now requires the reversal to penetrate six previous lows or highs. It is a much higher threshold than the standard setting of three previous lows or highs. At the same time, the time interval has dropped to one minute. This combination contributes to a stable visualization of the action. Even at the one-minute time interval, we can detect a persistence of bearish sentiment. The chart shows twenty-six consecutive one-minute new lows! The most interesting aspect of the six-line break is its ability to allow the trader to detect a stability and strength in the sentiment direction without the noise that usually accompanies one-minute candlestick charts.

Using a six-line break, the trader can enter the position with a market order. As a result, he will be joining the action, even though the trend has started to resume. There is a risk that the trade will be late. However, the idea is to ride the sentiment and stay in until either a limit is reached or a stop-loss is reached.

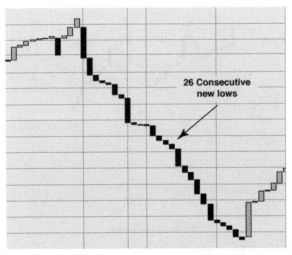

26 Consecutive new lows

Figure 4.5 Six-Line Break of GBPUSD Using One-Minute Chart (23/01/2009)

Let's explore how to determine stop-losses with price break charts. A feature of price break charts is their easy scalability across different time intervals. This means that price break charts apply to large time intervals as well as to time intervals of five minutes and one minute, and even apply at the tick level. With one-minute (and shorter) time frames, we can characterize the application as achieving microdetection of sentiment. This is unheard of with candlesticks. In Chapter 8, we focus on microdetection of sentiment through Renko charts, but price break charts also have this important characteristic. The benefit to the trader is that it allows detection of early signs of stability and instability in the sentiment of the moment.

When a trader who is trading in a high-momentum environment becomes profitable, the major questions become how far to ride the position and when to get out. A hyperaggressive trader could even consider using six-line one-second settings! The new low sequences had traveled twenty points and more. The interesting aspect of this setting is that even though it is at the micro level, a pattern of sentiment shows. It is not a coincidence: all trends start from a micro point.

Price Break and Tick-Level Price Action

With better data feeds and advanced interfaces, the trader can obtain high-frequency price data down to the tick level. A first reaction of many people is that at the tick level, there is too much noise. However, by using price break charts, we can filter out the noise and see patterns at the smallest possible levels.

The tick chart examples in **Figure 4.6** demonstrate that patterns are often embedded, even in tick-level data. We can see a clear sideways action in the equity Microsoft (MSFT). On a reversal up it generated twelve consecutive new highs in a row.

Six-Line Breaks and Fibs

Once again, we can apply Fibonacci resistance lines. In **Figure 4.7**, the high-to-low wave retraced with an initial six–line break setting. After drawing the Fibonacci resistance lines, the trader would see that the retracement broke through the 50 percent line. If the trader sought

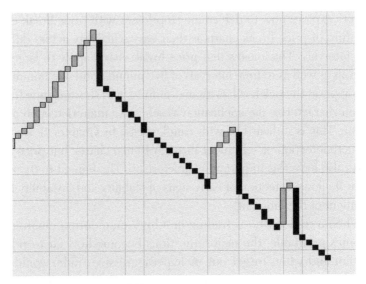

Figure 4.6 Tick Chart: MSFT

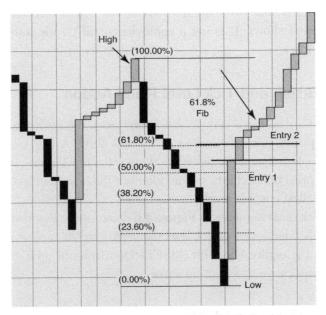

Figure 4.7 Fibonacci Resistance Line Applied to Six-Line Break Setting
Source: Chart copyright www.ProRealTime.com

more confirmation, he would see that when a new consecutive high appeared, it went through the 61.8 percent line. Entry at the break of this line would be an appropriate strategy.

CHAPTER 5

Channel Patterns, Cycles, and Price Breaks

WHEN A CHANNEL pattern appears in price data, it merits serious attention. Channel patterns show a persistence of sentiment in a unique way. Traders will notice that prices change within a channel. We can see in **Figure 5.1** that the price repeats a regular pattern of swings from high to low and low to high. We can therefore understand that channel patterns are really a form of cycles. This means that traders, when observing a channel pattern, should try to confirm whether there is a cycle

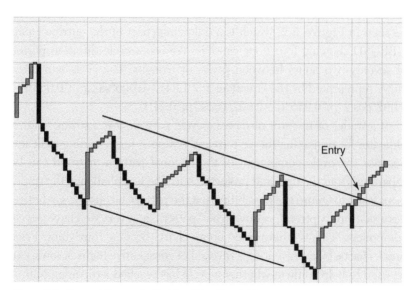

Figure 5.1 Channel Pattern in Six-Line Price Break Chart
Source: Abe Cofnas and Joseph Egbulefu

> As we know, the economy does not develop steadily and directly. In fact, it rises in cycles, that is, with expansion and contraction, or prosperity and slack, by turns. ... In order to effectively monitor and early-warn the macro economy, the economic cycle should be carefully examined.[1]

embedded in the pattern. Let's explore some further concepts underlying cycles. We will explore cycles with more depth in Chapter 13.

Cycles exist and express themselves everywhere. The lunar cycle is the most famous cycle, and is an almost perfect example of a pattern that we can accurately project into the future. We cannot project financial and market data with the same accuracy as a lunar cycle. It is still valid to investigate whether a cycle exists in the data, even if that cycle is not apparent. There should be no doubt that cycles are present in financial data. Some market data is very strongly cyclical and robust, while other market data can have intermittent cycles.

The persistence of embedded cycles in financial time series can be seen in **Figure 5.2**, which is a following chart of the currency pair GBPUSD showing four-hour candles. We see a cycle duration period of seventy-two hours between peaks or troughs. The cycle is a fitted curve represented by the equation: $Y = 1.641 - 0.006°\sin(2°pi°0.055°t) - 0.002°\cos(2°pi°0.055°t) - 0.002°\cos(2°pi°0.21°t)$.

If a trader or investor observes a cycle pattern, it is a strong leading indicator for projecting future tops and bottoms. It is a leading indicator because the cycle component of the channel pattern or trend can be separated from the data and projected out. The first challenge the trader faces is not to ignore the possibility that the pattern he observes, whether it is a sideways, uptrend, or downtrend pattern, may very well have a cycle component. This is where price break charts become important. Price break charts, by representing a reversal of consecutive highs or lows, can be used to help confirm whether a cycle has reached a turning point. A trader who combines cycle understanding and price break reversals has a powerful new tool for timing the market.

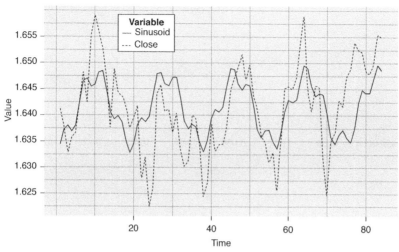

Figure 5.2 Cycle Turning Points in Four-Hour Candles
Source: Abe Cofnas and Joseph Egbulefu

Cycles and Price Break Charts

The combination of price break charts and cycles enables powerful new levels of confirmation. For example, the trader would look for cycle turning points coinciding with price break reversals or channel tops or bottoms. Notice how on November 2 and February 22, the cycle bottom coincided with a reversal up in the price break chart of the four-hour GBPUSD in **Figure 5.3**.

Where there is a coincidence of price breaks with cyclical turning points, the trade has very strong confirmation for a top or a bottom. The best approach is to start with raw price data and generate a chart. It can be a line or candlestick type, depending on the use of the chart. Survey data and economic data would be line data, because they have no open, high, low, or close. Price data would be candlestick data because it reflects trading behavior.

We can then generate a price break chart that transforms the data into points of consecutive new highs or consecutive new lows and reversals. We want to know if the reversals are co-aligned with a projected cycle turning point. This combination of price breaks and cycle or channel patterns takes price break charting to a new level of use. If the price break charts coincide with the data, we have unprecedented

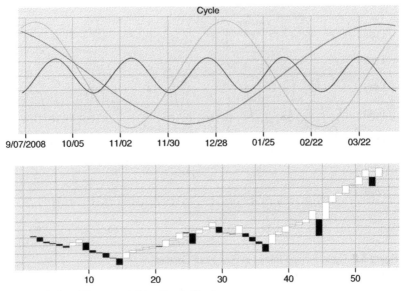

Figure 5.3 Sine Waves and Price Break Charts
Source: Abe Cofnas and Joseph Egbulefu

confirmation that a break in the trend or a projected price break reversal coincides with a peak or valley in a cycle that the price is in.

The question is, how can the average trader use this approach?

Several types of software for detecting if a data series exhibits cycle behavior are now available. In the coming years, many cycle indicators will be forthcoming as cycle science improves with new techniques of detection. A more detailed analysis of the cycle indicator is the subject of Chapter 13.

Chapter Note

1.   Proceedings of 2007 IEEE International Conference on Grey Systems and Intelligent Services, November 18–20, 2007, Nanjing, China.

CHAPTER 6

Multiple Market Applications of Price Break Charts

TRADERS CAN USE PRICE break chart events in one market as leading indicators for directional moves in another market. This makes sense when markets' movements are highly correlated. Many of these intermarket comparisons have cycles of correlation. At times, the correlations, measured by R squared, may be in the 90s, while at other times they may disconnect. If the correlation data is accessible, it is a good idea for the trader to check the status of the daily correlations.

Contemporaneous Visual Correlation of Instruments

One conventional approach is to use what can be called *contemporaneous visual correlation*. This involves scanning the charts of both instruments to determine visually if their movements are synchronous. There are many examples of such correlations.

S&P 500, Dow, Cash, and USDJPY

The relationship between the equity markets and the yen, shown in **Figure 6.1**, is an important intermarket correlation that traders follow. These correlations can reach over 90 percent. Sometimes the S&P 500 leads the way, and at other times, the yen leads the way.

Generally, the expressed sentiment relates to global risk aversion or risk appetite. When the U.S. equity markets are attractive, they act as a

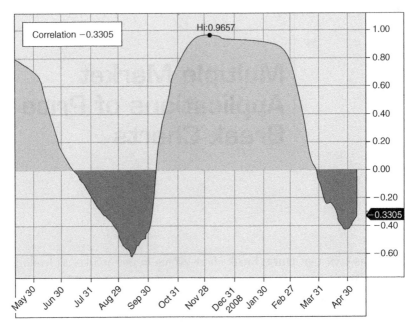

Figure 6.1 S&P 500/Yen Line Chart
Source: Bloomberg

magnet for capital. As a result, yen investors borrow yen at near-zero interest rates and leverage their yen into other assets, namely U.S. markets. The correlations are very close, as can be seen in the chart in **Figure 6.2**. The trader trading one of these markets would look at price break charts to determine (1) where a projected break reversal point would be, and (2) if there were any breaks in earlier time intervals that could prove to be a signal that the sentiment was changing. The general strategy of borrowing from currencies that have very low interest rates and investing the borrowed capital in assets to seek a higher return is known as the Carry Trade. In recent years, the yen was the favored currency of borrowing. Since the decline of U.S. interest rates to levels of 0.25 percent, the U.S. dollar is a candidate for replacing the yen as the carry trade borrowed currency.

A review of price break charts of the SPX shows that on March 9, 2009, at the low of 676, the price break charts projected that 700.82 (reached earlier on March 2), if penetrated above, would constitute a

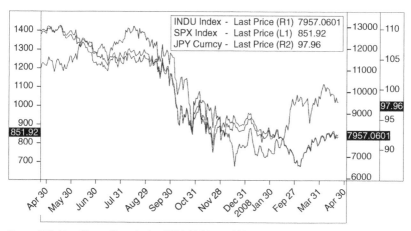

Figure 6.2 Line Chart Correlating SPX, DJIA, and Yen
Source: Bloomberg

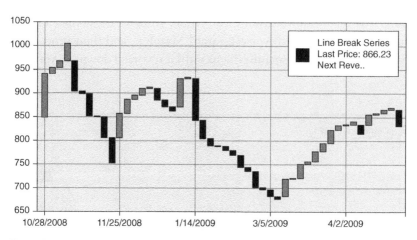

Figure 6.3 SPX Price Break Chart
Source: Bloomberg

reversal of sentiment. This happened on March 10, when a high of 719.6 was reached, resulting in several up columns (**Figure 6.3**).

Now let's integrate this information and formulate a trading strategy. The trader would take the projected reversal point of 700.82 as an alert for a shift in sentiment to a buy dollar and sell yen position, because a reversal to bullish sentiment in the SPX translates to a dollar bull environment. After the SPX reversed on May 10, permission to look for a buy setup on the USDJPY was in effect based on the USDJPY price break charts.

Copper and Freeport–McMoRan Copper and FCX

Equity traders can use the intermarket correlations of an equity with its sector and apply price break charts as well. **Figures 6.4–6.7** present an example using copper futures and share prices of the leading copper mining company, Freeport–McMoRan. They are without doubt synchronous. The equity trader can use price breaks on both charts and verify whether to be bullish or bearish or stay neutral. The FCX price break chart showed a reversal on February 5, with a new high close of 26.35. It subsequently went to sixteen new consecutive highs until it reversed down again on April 20. In contrast, copper on the futures market didn't reverse up until March 5, and then proceeded to register eleven consecutive highs until it reversed down on April 20.

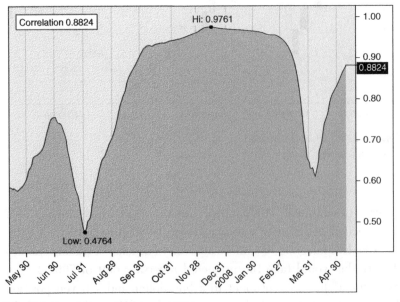

Figure 6.4 Correlation of Copper and FCX

Source: Bloomberg

Figure 6.5 Copper versus Freeport McMoRan
Source: Bloomberg

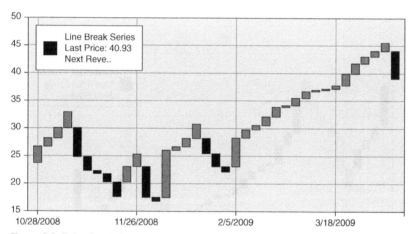

Figure 6.6 Price Break Chart of FCX
Source: Bloomberg

In this case, the FCX price break chart reversal was a leading indicator for the copper futures reversal, which we see clearly in **Figure 6.7**.

Volatility and Price Break Charts

An index that is very important to traders is the VIX volatility index. It is understood to provide a gauge of fear in the market. The VIX's patterns are a core part of many trading strategies. When volatility increases, selling is a favored option strategy. When volatility decreases, it favors

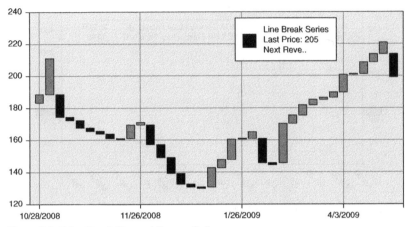

Figure 6.7 Price Break Chart of Copper Daily
Source: Bloomberg

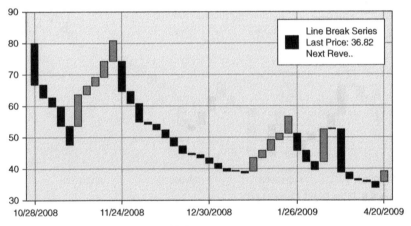

Figure 6.8 Price Break Chart of VIX Index
Source: Bloomberg

option buyers. The VIX is, not surprisingly, often highly correlated with the USDJPY pair. In the period from May 12, 2008 to May 11, 2009, the VIX reached a –0.95 correlation with the USDJPY pair. In other words, when the VIX is low, the USDJPY moves up.

If the VIX is a leading indicator for movements in the USDJPY or other instruments, what happens when we look at the VIX from a price break chart perspective (**Figures 6.8–6.9**)? The trader can clearly

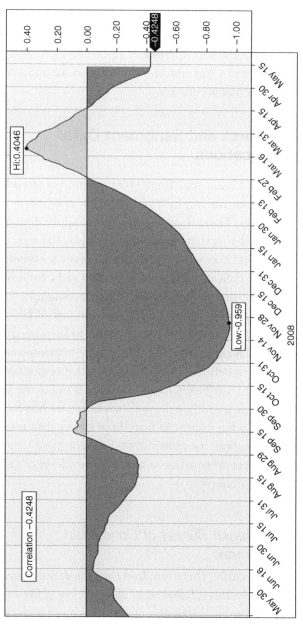

Figure 6.9 VIX Index and USDJPY Correlations

Source: Bloomberg

discern moods of the market. A sequence of declining steps in the VIX price break chart shows fear declining, while a sequence of new highs shows fear increasing.

In short, the inter-market correlations provide a "proximity alert." In other words, when one market experiences a price break or generates a detectable alert, the trader can consider this an alert for an impending reversal in the market that is correlated.

Price Break Charts and Sentiment Data: Innovative Applications

Traders usually think of using price break charts to interpret trend direction and strength when trading instruments such as equities, bonds, indexes, and currencies. There is another important application of price break charts analysis that is virtually unknown. This is the use of price break charts to interpret consumer and business survey sentiment data. Consumer sentiment data and business sentiment data have become increasingly important inputs that central banks, economists, and the markets use to assess economic and market conditions. When survey information comes out, markets move in response to surprise data that indicates there is a change in attitude. The survey responses are presented as the difference between positive and negative responses. Then they are converted into a *diffusion index*. The data is not in the form of open, high, low, and close. Although candlesticks are useless for diffusion index–type data, a line chart can map these survey data results. In a breakthrough application, we transformed the sentiment data into a three-line price break chart to arrive at an entire new level of granularity. Let's look at some examples.

University of Michigan Survey of Consumer Confidence Sentiment

This survey occurs monthly. Three hundred consumers are interviewed as a preliminary sample; this is followed by an interview of five hundred persons. The survey combines attitudes about the present with expectations regarding future economic conditions. Until recently, the data was always presented as a line chart. As of this writing, the survey results showed lows that were unprecedented (**Figure 6.10**). The latest data

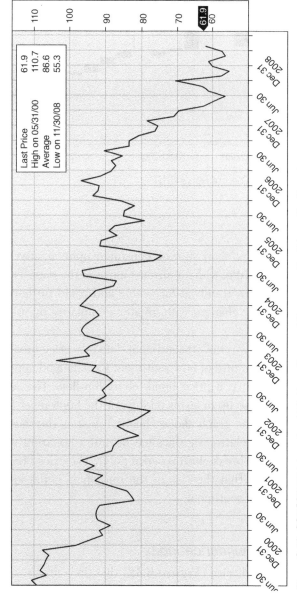

Last Price	61.9
High on 05/31/00	110.7
Average	86.6
Low on 11/30/08	55.3

Figure 6.10 CONSSENT–University of Michigan Survey of Consumer Confidence Sentiment

Source: Bloomberg

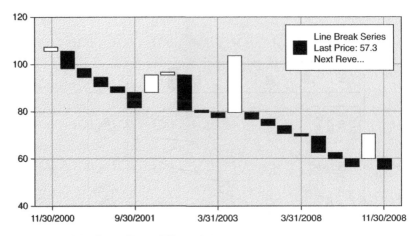

Figure 6.11 Price Break Chart of Figure 6.10
Source: Bloomberg

when viewed as a line chart showed consumer opinion survey results that appeared optimistic, with an upward move in the data. The trader shouldn't take the raw results at face value and could further confirm the consumer survey changes with greater granularity by using price break charts.

Therefore, when we convert sentiment data into price break charts, an unprecedented picture of how sentiment has changed appears. We can see that there was a price break chart flip-flop. The sentiment would need to reverse up to levels taking out the September 30, 2008 high of 70.3. The line graph shows the 70.3 area as the most recent high peak, but its relative significance becomes apparent when we perceive it as a price break chart reversal point. The price break chart, **Figure 6.11**, shows that the rise in the line chart is not enough to register a reversal of sentiment.

ZEW German Confidence Index

This is a monthly indicator (**Figure 6.12**) that presents the results of a survey of nearly 350 institutional investors and analysts about future economic conditions in Germany. Notice that the price break chart in **Figure 6.13** shows an upward break in the sentiment has occurred. The question is, will it last?

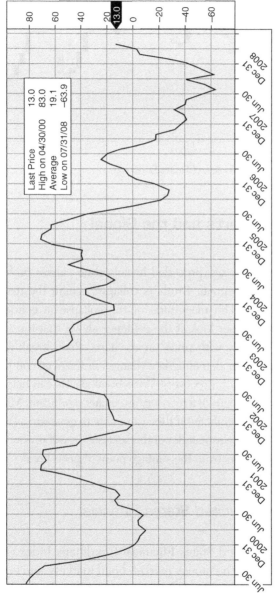

Figure 6.12 ZEW German Confidence Index Monthly Chart

Source: Bloomberg

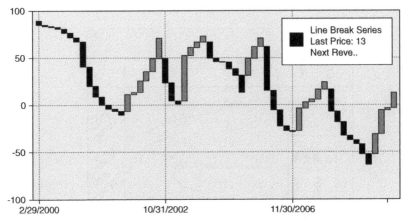

Figure 6.13 Price Break Version of Figure 6.12

Source: Bloomberg

Price Break Charts and the Global Financial Crises

The global financial crises, preceded by subprime market problems and precipitated by the Lehman Brothers collapse, caught the markets and experts by surprise. The magnitude of the collapse in conditions was unprecedented. A closer look at the evidence shows that the signs were detectable, particularly with price break charts. Price break charts also can be a useful tool for detecting key changes in financial conditions and monitoring the status of a recovery. Price break charts can help pinpoint whether incremental signs of a recovery are in fact significant. Many would consider these signs significant if they were able to generate a price break chart reversal up. In the remainder of this section, we will review key financial condition indicators from the vantage point of price break charts.

The Bloomberg United States Financial Conditions Index

The Bloomberg United States Financial Conditions Index (BFCIUS) reflects conditions in the money market, bond markets, and equity markets. **Figure 6.14** shows the dramatic upheaval that the financial crises engendered.

The index values are standard deviations from a normal condition. On February 22, 2007, the BFCIUS hit a high score at a level of 1.198 Z.

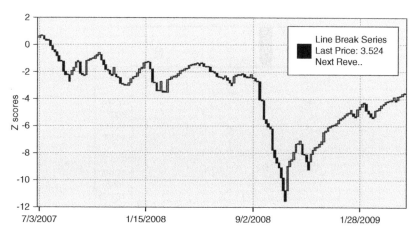

Figure 6.14 BFCIUS Bloomberg United States Financial Conditions Index
Source: Bloomberg

Z is a statistical term representing the number of standard deviations past the mean. This meant that financial conditions were about 70 percent above the mean or normal score. (One standard deviation represents 67 percent deviation.) We can see that financial conditions began deteriorating. On September 1, the BFCIUS Index was –2.303. Then the bottom fell out and on October 10, 2008, the BFCIUS Index hit a low of –11.551! This represents a probabililty of "1 in 10 octillion where 1 octillion can be represented as 1 followed by 27 zeros." (Source: http://www.trilogyadvisors.com/worldreport/200910.Lehman.pdf.) Thereafter the line chart shows a slow upward move and a return to pre-crisis conditions.

Price break chart analysis shows some interesting aspects of the movement toward recovery. First, conditions of recovery are wavelike. The initial upward move in the index after October's 10 lows involved seven consecutive highs. Then a pullback of four consecutive lows occurred, taking the index back to –9.21 on November 20, 2008. However, after this point a break reversal up included twenty consecutive new highs, reaching a level of –4.801 on January 13, 2009. At that time recovery stalled, and created a support area at –3.59.

Does price break chart analysis confirm the recovery in financial conditions? Let's take a look.

The price break chart in Figure 6.14 points to a small incremental sequence of higher scores on business conditions. The angle of the

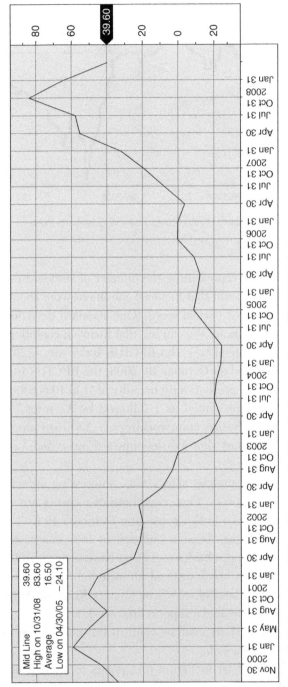

Figure 6.15 Senior Loan Officers Opinion on Bank Lending Practices Survey (SLDETIGT Index)

Source: Bloomberg

increase is about 45 degrees, which confirms an overall confidence in improved conditions. Of additional interest is the fact that reversals down were quite limited in distance.

Senior Loan Officers Survey

A very important survey related to monitoring financial conditions is the Senior Loan Officers Opinion on Bank Lending Practices Survey. The Federal Reserve conducts this survey and issues this report (SLDETIGT Index), which tracks attitudes of key bank officers regarding whether lending practices are becoming tighter or looser. This type of report is implemented in several countries. Traders who want to obtain an in-depth understanding of financial conditions, and perhaps a leading indicator of changes in financial conditions, should access those reports. The two charts represented in **Figures 6.15** and **6.16** represent the supply and demand for credit. They track whether conditions for commercial and industrial loans were tightening, and whether the demand for commercial and industrial loans was increasing or decreasing. It is significant to note that credit conditions were breaking into new areas of tightening in 2007, and that tightening standards went parabolic in the late summer of 2008. On the demand side, the demand for commercial and industrial loans peaked in 2005.

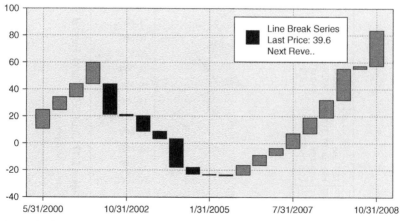

Figure 6.16 Price Break Version of Figure 6.15

Source: Bloomberg

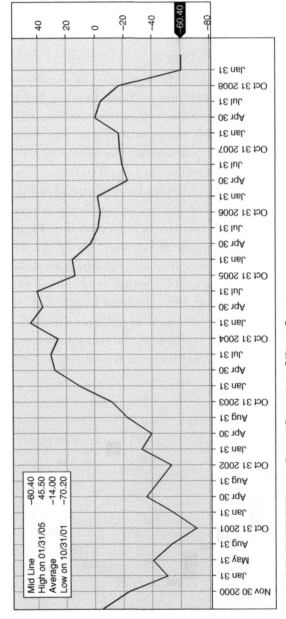

Figure 6.17 SLDEDEMD Index–Federal Senior Loan Officers Survey

Source: Bloomberg

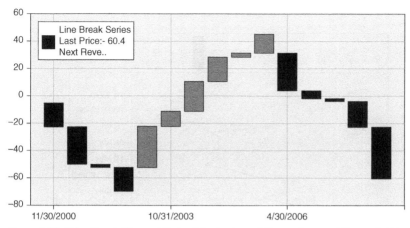

Figure 6.18 Price Break Chart of Federal Senior Loan Officers Survey of Figure 6.17

Source: Bloomberg

The price break chart in Figure 6.16 demonstrates that conditions of tightening on commercial and industrial loans experienced a major reversal in the beginning of 2006 and continued to tighten in a sequence of nine new consecutive high closes on the survey. As of May 2009, the line chart shows a dip in tightening, but the price break chart doesn't register this as big enough to generate a reversal column.

On the demand side, we show the result of the survey on the net percentage of domestic respondents reporting stronger demand for commercial and industrial loans for large and medium-sized firms (SLDEDEMD Index). The line chart in **Figure 6.17** and the price break version in **Figure 6.18** show that the decline was in the making years in advance of the financial crises. It also shows a flattening or bottoming out of the negative spiral. Is this significant?

Philadelphia Federal Reserve Bank Business Outlook Survey

The Philadelphia Fed Business Outlook Survey provides another look at business conditions. Both the line chart **(Figure 6.19)** and the price break chart **(Figure 6.20)** show volatility in the responses. There is a glimmer of a respite in negative responses, as the last two consecutive lows registered very flat in shape. This shows a dissipation of energy.

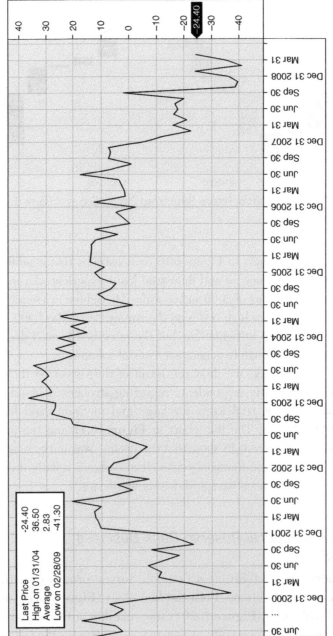

Figure 6.19 Philadelphia Federal Reserve Business Outlook Survey Diffusion Index General Conditions

Source: Bloomberg

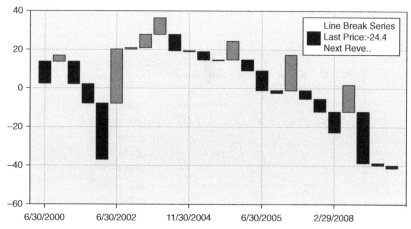

Figure 6.20 Price Break Version of Figure 6.19
Source: Bloomberg

The Milwaukee Purchasers Manufacturing Index

This index is a monthly survey of purchasers, and provides a gauge of expectations in the manufacturing sector. The line chart (**Figure 6.21**) showed a bounce up at the latest view. Was it significant? From a price break perspective, a reversal column up did not yet register (**Figure 6.22**).

By reviewing price break displays of important measures of financial recovery it should be clear that price break charts make it easier to detect whether progress toward a recovery is occurring as well as monitoring the strength of a potential recovery. When price break reversals occur among financial recovery indicators they are of paramount importance for confirming that a change in the financial condition has occurred.

Price Break Charts and Inflation Watching

Inflation watching is a byproduct of financial condition recovery watching. Price break charts can be especially valuable to traders looking for signs of inflation. Let's use the RJ/DRB Commodity Price Index (CRY) (**Figure 6.23**) as a gauge of inflationary expectations, because this index presents an arithmetic average of commodity prices. Inflation, if it recurs, will appear as a signature of a breakout in the CRY. The price break chart in **Figure 6.24** shows that a reversal above the 229 level

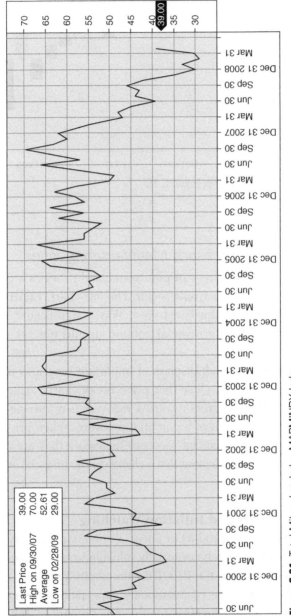

Figure 6.21 Total Milwaukee Index-MAPMINDX Index

Source: Bloomberg

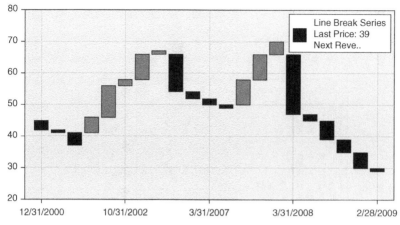

Figure 6.22 Price Break Version of Figure 6.21 MAPMINDX Index
Source: Bloomberg

occurred, indicating that reversal toward bullish sentiment occurred on March 23. A play on expectation of inflation would therefore focus on the CRY staying above this price area.

German Business Expectations

The German economy is the key driver in the eurozone economy. When results of business expectation surveys appear, they are highly relevant as indicators and can affect the market. Do price break charts provide added value to the analysis of these surveys?

Notice the movement of the sentiment data for the EURUSD currency pair **(Figure 6.25)**. The currencies are in general synchronicity. The upturn in sentiment seems strong, but it is difficult to assess the degree of reversal of sentiment from a deep decline to a positive attitude.

A scan of the price break chart of the IFO Pan German Business Expectations Index, GRIFPEX Index **(Figure 6.26)** provides additional insight. The upturn in sentiment in the line chart does not register enough to create a price break, but the trader knows exactly where the price break will occur. Count back three lines and you have a price break point of 86. That would signal a significant break in the downward sentiment.

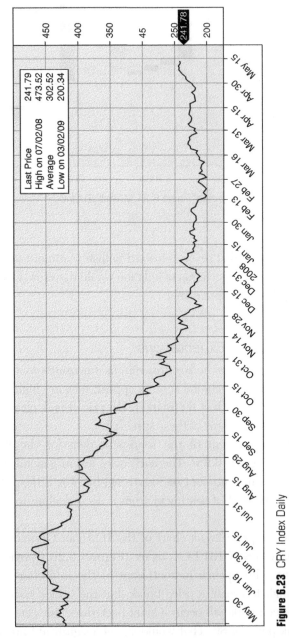

Figure 6.23 CRY Index Daily

Source: Bloomberg

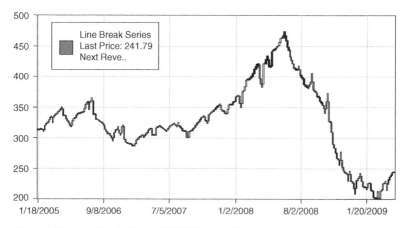

Figure 6.24 Price Break Chart of CRY Figure 6.23
Source: Bloomberg

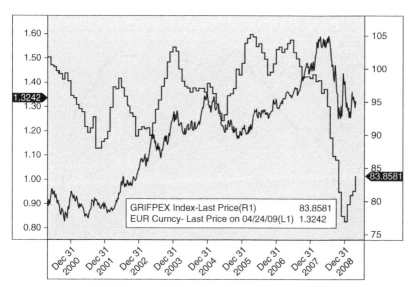

FIGURE 6.25 IFO Pan German Business Expectations Index and EURUSD
Source: Bloomberg

Japan Tankan Survey of Business Conditions

This survey is a comprehensive survey of over ten thousand companies that are asked whether business conditions will improve. If you look at **Figure 6.27**, it won't take long to see the depression in business sentiment about conditions in Japan. The question facing the analyst or

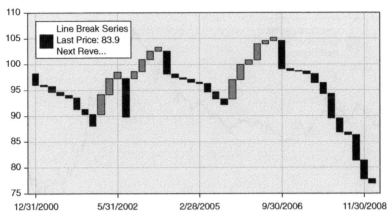

FIGURE 6.26 Price Break Chart of GRIFPEX Index

Source: Bloomberg

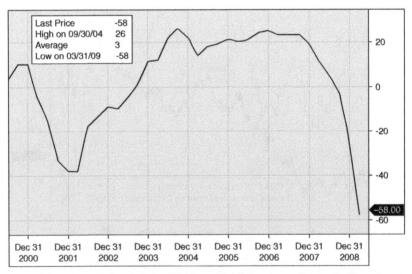

Figure 6.27 Japan Tankan Survey of Business Conditions Large Enterprises Manufacturing (JNTSMFG Index)

Source: Bloomberg

observer of Japanese business conditions is, "When would an increase in positive sentiment be considered significant?" The price break chart in **Figure 6.28** indicates that it would be significant when the survey results continue for three lines (a value of 6).

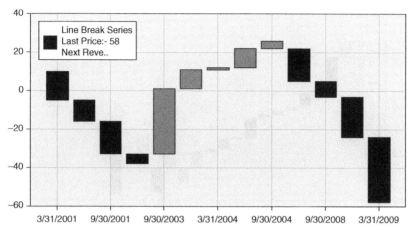

Figure 6.28 Price Break Version of JNTSMFG Index, Figure 6.27

Source: Bloomberg

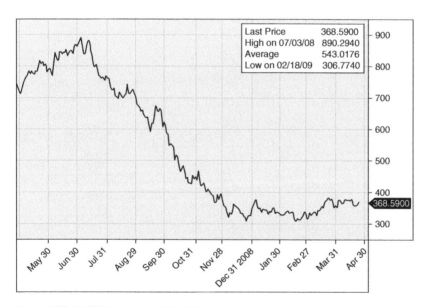

Figure 6.29 SPGSCI Index-The S&P GSCI Index

Source: Bloomberg

Commodity Markets and Price Break Charts

The global financial contraction has severely affected the commodity markets. The S&P GSCI Index provides a monitor of expectations. The line chart **(Figure 6.29)** shows a slow cup inverse arc moving up. The price break chart **(Figure 6.30)** reveals a choppy quality and the need to wait for a reversal.

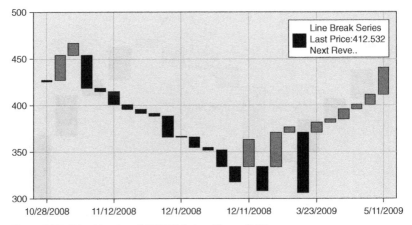

Figure 6.30 Price Version of SPGSCI Index, Figure 6.29

Source: Bloomberg

CHAPTER 7

Price Break Charts and Option Trading

PRICE BREAK CHARTS can assist the trader in deriving option trading strategies and tactics. The option trader is essentially making a directional decision on the trade. He anticipates the move based on his evaluation of market conditions, and the strength of that evaluation will essentially determine the outcome. This is in contrast to the spot trader, who reacts to the action and tries to join a move. Since the proposed option trade is either a pattern or trend continuation trade or one that anticipates a reversal of the trend, price break charts can become a key tool in confirming the strength of that analysis. Additionally, once the anticipated direction is established, the trader needs to select the strike prices. Price break charts offer a methodology for choosing the strike price locations. This chapter will explore innovative uses of price break charts in option trading.

Selecting Direction with Price Break Charts

An option trader's first priority is to establish a direction for a trade. Being wrong on the underlying direction will reduce the probability of being in a winnable option trade. A trader can make this directional decision in many ways, but we will focus on price break charts as a useful tool for selecting direction. Tom DeMark, a noted leader in technical analysis, writes in his book, *DeMark on Day Trading Options* about rules for buying calls and puts.

> **Rule No. 1:** Buy calls when the overall market is down; buy puts when the overall market is up.[1]

Rule No. 2: Buy calls when the industry group is down; buy puts when the industry group is up.

Rule No. 3: Buy calls when the underlying security is down; buy puts when the underlying security is up.

The application of these rules with price break charts is nearly perfect. Let's give them a price break charts perspective.

Rules for Buying Calls and Puts with Price Break Charts

Rule No. 1: Buy calls when the overall market is down and the day price break is in a sequence of consecutive lows.

Rule No. 2: Buy calls when the industry group is down and the day price break of a key industry index is in a sequence of consecutive lows.

Rule No. 3: Buy calls when the underlying security is down and the day price break is showing consecutive lows; buy puts when the underlying security is up and the day price break of that security is showing consecutive highs.

What price break charting does is calibrate the trader's ability to implement Tom DeMark's rules. It also goes further and helps the trader select the strike price location for the call or put.

Selecting the Strike Price

Once the trader selects a direction, the critical next step is to identify which strike price to put on the trade. There are several considerations to assess. First, how far should the strike price be from current market prices? A strike price close to the money will be expensive, but will have a higher percentage move with the price (known as the delta). A strike price further away from the money will be less expensive, but the sensitivity of the option price movement to the underlying price also will be less. Can price break charts help in deciding on strike price location? Let's explore how they can.

Price break charts give powerful criteria for selecting an option strike price, and can be particularly useful for spread positions. The reason they can be of great significance is that there is maximum sentiment expression or force at the moment of a price reversal. Remember that the criterion for a reversal using three-line price break chart settings is that the sentiment was powerful enough to take out the three previous highs or lows. This phenomenon suggests that price break chart points are natural locations for strike prices.

Let's look at the S&P 500 cash index using three-line weekly price break chart settings and see what it suggests regarding selecting a strike price. An initial scan of **Figure 7.1** suggests that the direction is down, with two attempts to reverse back up.

We can confirm either a bullish or a bearish strategy by using price break charts. Consider that on May 20, 2008, the S&P had just set two consecutive highs in a row. A trader looking to play a reversal in an option play would locate three previous low closes. This line would be the location for the strike price for a put position. The expiration date can vary, but a three-month duration would be acceptable and would give time for the market sentiment to reverse and move down further.

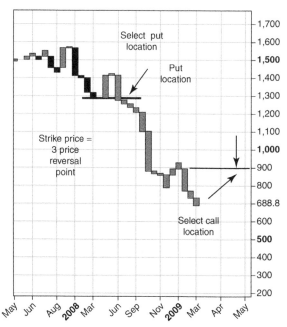

Figure 7.1 Option Strategy Using Price Break Charts
Source: Chart copyright www.ProRealTime.com

In March 2009, the S&P 500 was down with three consecutive lows. Therefore, a trader playing a bullish reversal would have counted back three consecutive highs and selected 900 as the strike price.

Figure 7.1 thereby illustrates how both strategies can use price break charts as a guide to strike price selection.

Variations in price break chart settings allow strategies and tactics for shorter option plays. Taking the same S&P data, let's look at the day chart from a six-line price break chart perspective. Shifting to the six-line price break chart gives the trader a very clear confirmation that there is a stability in the sentiment. The bearish sentiment is quantifiable, with powerful sequences of consecutive new lows and intermittent retracements. A trader looking to be bearish on an options play would like the conditions depicted in **Figure 7.2**. The price action demonstrates a retracement up with eight consecutive new day highs. The trader would count back six lines to 829.39 and select a strike price right below it for selling a put. If the trader was also considering a spread, the location of the other side of the spread for buying a put would be at 675.

An interesting aspect of the six-line price break chart setting appears when traders play a potential flip-flop. As we indicated in an earlier chapter, this occurs when a reversal column reverses immediately back again. With a six-line break setting, we can assume that there is a great

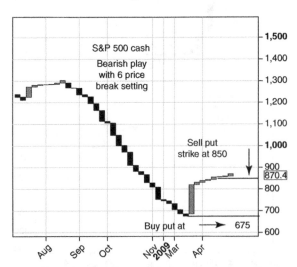

Figure 7.2 S&P 500 Cash: Bearish Play with Six-Line Price Break Setting

Source: Chart copyright www.ProRealTime.com

deal of momentum coming with the second reversal back. The Gold price action, which **Figure 7.3** illustrates with a six-line price break chart, has witnessed several of these flip-flops, demonstrating an option trading opportunity.

The general strategy is as follows: Once a reversal column appears, place a one-month-away option, playing a reversal again back to the origin of the move. A flip-flop will be powerful enough to continue with consecutive highs on a reversal back up, or consecutive lows on a reversal down.

On November 19, 2007, gold closed at 781.75 and generated a down reversal column. The trader would play a flip-flop by putting on a gold call at the projected reversal point of 833.59, which was the previous high. Remember that a six-line reversal had occurred down; an immediate six-line reversal up would take the price to the high that had occurred right before the reversal. In this case, the strike price one or two months out would be 835. The flip-flop occurred on December 28, 2008 at 840.5 and proceeded to move in twelve consecutive highs to a high of 929.40 on January 30, 2009. The central idea is to use the projected six-price reversal point as an entry location.

Risk Reversal Price Break Charts Analysis for Currency Traders

The risk reversals (also known as the 25 Delta R/R) relating to a currency pair comprise a special set of data that is important to currency traders. The risk reversal is the implied volatility of the 25-delta call

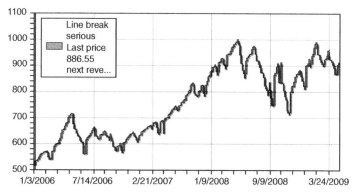

Figure 7.3 Six-Line Price Break Chart Reversal and Gold Option Trading
Source: Bloomberg

minus the implied volatility of the 25-delta put. Theoretically, if the market were neutral in sentiment on the direction, the implied volatilities would be the same. If the market favors one direction over the other, then the implied volatility of one 25-delta option (put or call) will be higher than that of the other. Often, the market skews in one direction. The degree of the skew is called a *risk reversal*. For the purposes of this book, risk reversals (RRs) are important because they often correlate with the direction of the underlying spot position. Essentially, RRs mirror market sentiment relating to the direction of the spot. We can see this in the chart of the AUDUSD currency pair overlaid with its risk reversals **(Figure 7.4)**.

Serious forex option traders pay close attention to risk reversals as a directional indicator. There are two risk reversal strategies to employ. The first one is to go with the flow; if the smile is skewed one way, the direction of your next option trade should be, if this strategy is followed, in the direction of the skew. On the other hand, there may be times when the skew is very extreme, and at those moments, a strategy of trading in the reverse direction could be justified. In both cases, price break charts help. In the first scenario (trading in the direction of the skew), converting the RR line chart to a price break chart will indicate if the RR wave has in fact significantly reversed its direction. It is always better to ride the RR wave when it begins, as that is when there is strong trend sentiment. Price break charts help identify such a beginning. Playing a contrarian move would also be easier to implement with a price break chart, because the price break patterns would indicate whether the RR direction is becoming tired. If so, going against it may simply be anticipating an impending reversal.

Let's look again at the AUDUSD currency pair and its risk reversal chart. There is a close relationship between the RRs and the spot price movements. A trader who looks to the RR to decide in which direction to trade would have a high level of confidence that the RR chart is a powerful clue. Even greater confidence is achieved by converting the RR chart into its own price break chart. The resulting price break chart provides increased detail as to when there would be a change in direction and where it would occur. In **Figure 7.5**, which is the price break chart version of the RR chart in Figure 7.4, the reversal up on Dec 15th signaled that the option sentiment had changed from a trend of consecutive lower RR levels, showing a favoring of put. The reversal

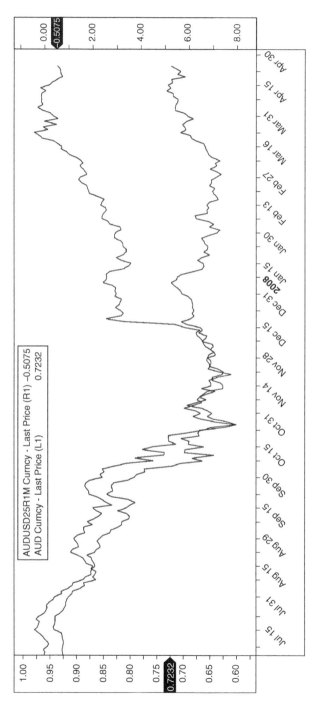

Figure 7.4 Line Chart of AUDUSD Risk Reversals

Source: Bloomberg

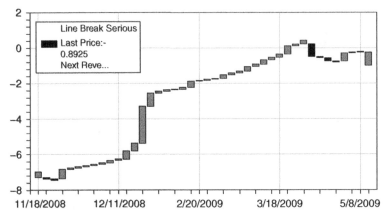

Figure 7.5 Price Break Chart of AUDUSD Risk Reversals

Source: Bloomberg

up, while still showing negative RR levels demonstrated a change in the tone of the sentiment. Using the price break chart reversal meant that going short on the AUDUSD was no longer supported by the risk reversal price break charts. Additionally, a trader following the RR logic and going long on the AUDUSD on Dec 15th, would have witnessed a sustained rise in the AUDUSD from approximately .70 on Dec 15th to .95 in March. On March 26th the AUDUSD25R1M price break chart reversed down for an exit signal. The price break signals provided the ability to ride the action to over 2000 pips.

We can look at the EURJPY currency pair as another example of how a price break view of the RR curve is helpful. First, we can see that there is a strong co-movement of the spot and the RR. The RR chart **(Figure 7.6)** shows a leveling off of the option sentiment that had favored the call side. Should the trader consider puts? The next step would be to see if the price break version of the RR **(Figure 7.7)** shows a reversal. It does! This would be a confirming signal to sell.

Price Breaks and Currency Volatility Smiles

Another way to use price break charting with currency option trading is to apply it to volatility smiles. The term *volatility smile* refers to the shape of the curve generated by the implied volatility at different delta strike prices. These smiles are considered important in currency

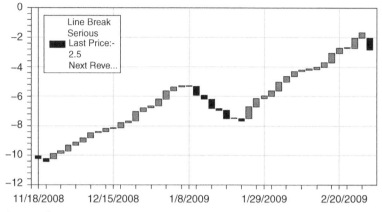

Figure 7.6 EURJPY Risk Reversal Curve

Source: Bloomberg

markets. Theoretically, there should be a simple smile where the market has no bias in direction. But markets can be skewed, and when you see a volatility smirk leaning to one direction, it shows that sentiment is biased for calls or puts. The trader's challenge is to interpret the volatility smile. Is it leading or lagging? Is it overextended? By using price break charting in relationship to volatility smiles, the trader can get a handle on whether the smile shape is also confirming a reversal.

For example, consider the volatility smile in **Figure 7.8a**, which shows option opinion leaning to the call side. An option trader looking at this chart may consider placing calls on the EURUSD pair. An alternative view would be to consider the smile to be overextended and buy a put playing the opposite view. Here is where price break charts can make a difference and augment the decision process. The price break chart of the EURUSD **(Figure 7.8b)** shows that there is a reversal break downward, with two consecutive new day lows. It is probable that a trader using these price break results would conclude that the smile was not likely to last, because the price break direction did not confirm it.

Consider the example of the currency pair AUDUSD. In **Figure 7.9a**, we see a volatility smile that is heavily skewed to the put side. Traders call this a *smirk*. In fact, it is very severe. Based on this chart, a trader could conclude that going with the option opinion was the way

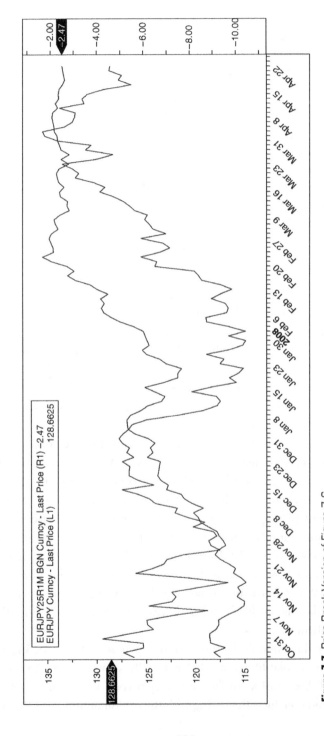

Figure 7.7 Price Break Version of Figure 7.6

Source: Bloomberg

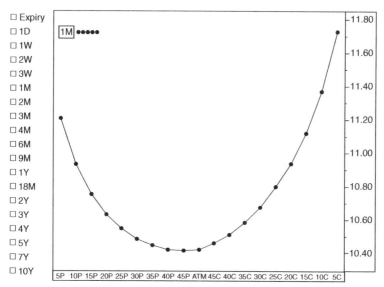

Figure 7.8a Volatility Smile of EURUSD

Source: Bloomberg

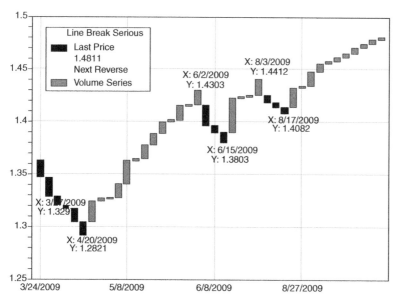

Figure 7.8b Price Break Chart of EURUSD

Source: Bloomberg

to go, and so he would place a put on the AUDUSD. However, the price break chart in **Figure 7.9b** shows that the AUD is still in a long sequence of new highs. In this case, the smile is opposite the trend direction and may be leading it. But there are interesting clues in the price break chart. Notice that the size of the price break high sequences are getting short, almost flat. This indicates a tired trend. If the trader was to put on a put anticipating a reversal, he would count back 3 lines from

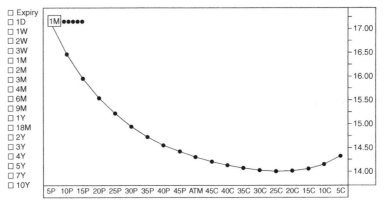

Figure 7.9a AUDUSD Smirk

Source: Bloomberg

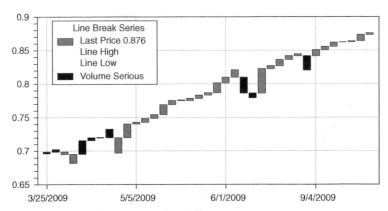

Figure 7.9b AUDUSD Three-Line Break Chart

Source: Bloomberg

the latest low and use that point as a nearby strike price. On Figure 7.9b that point is .8624. Therefore .86 would be a desireable strike location for a put.

Chapter Note

1.   McGraw-Hill, 1999.

CHAPTER 8

Renko Charts
Revived
The Microdetection
of Sentiment

"TAKING INTO ACCOUNT the characteristics and behaviors of one's adversary is essential for success in any competitive activity, such as in sports, business, or warfare."[1]

People have used many metaphors to describe trading. They have referred to trading as a "war" in which there is a battle between bulls and bears. Within the military mind-set, the trader can be a warrior, gladiator, or sniper. We often hear sports metaphors; for example, traders are likened commonly to surfers. All of these metaphors are important because they provide insights not only into how traders act, but also into how they learn, and improve, their trading.

Traders bring metaphors about trading from their own life experiences. Engineers try to model the market. Doctors try to diagnose the patterns. Musicians attempt to listen to the market's rhythms. All of these are valid and help the trader. When it comes to the phase of trading that deals with protecting profits, the trader enters a zone of combat, so the adversarial metaphor works well. The role of the profitable trader is to protect his profits, and the weapon is Renko bricks.

Before we focus on Renko bricks, let's quickly review where we just left off: price break charts.

We applied price break charts to detecting the beginning of a trend. Their essential feature is their ability to project the resumption of a trend after a retracement. To a great extent, price break charts improve strategies and tactics for entering a trade. This is because entry decisions require more planning, and the trader has time to evaluate a great many conditions existing when the trade is put on. Now, let's look at the opposite side of the trader's decision path and focus on another of the highest priorities of a trader: determining when to get *out* of a position. If the position is losing money, using traditional stop-loss positions to get out and minimize losses has been, though imperfect, an accepted practice. There is a rich set of technical indicators that help traders exit a position. So now we come to a defining point in the trader's theatre of action: how to get out when the position is profitable. Even a small improvement in a trader's ability to stay in a profitable position can have a large impact on profitability.

The focus of this chapter is the specific challenge of exiting a position after the position becomes profitable. Seeing profits emerge on a trade excites the trader, and there is a propensity to take the profit. This desire to capture early profits presents problems to the trader, because it prevents improvements in trading efficiency. Even good traders leave money "on the table." The psychological challenge is not to give in to one's fear of losing the profits. The technical challenge is to recognize when conditions require lightening up on a position—or getting out— before the position turns from a profit to a loss.

These challenges are real. If you ask your trader friends what methods and criteria they use to exit a profitable position, you will receive a wide variety of answers. This chapter sheds new light on exiting profitable positions by using Renko chart-based charting and analysis.

What is Renko Charting?

Renko charting is a tool that represents price movements by using bricks. Renko is the Japanese word for *brick*. If a price has moved higher by a prescribed amount, we add a new brick. We can select the color; it is usually green, white, or gray. If the price has moved lower by a prescribed amount, a new block, whose color is usually either black or red, appears in the opposite direction.

The computational logic for constructing a Renko chart, shown here and illustrated as a flowchart in **Figures 8.1** and **8.2**, is used to create Renko charts in most programs. It follows the rules set forth in the book *Beyond Candlesticks*, which we discussed in Chapter 2.

The essence of Renko charting is that each brick reveals, at various time intervals, key information on market sentiment. Renko bricks become

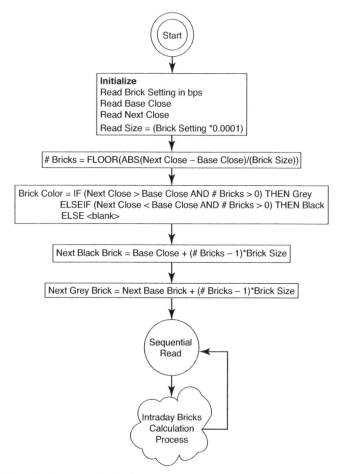

Figure 8.1 Renko Construction Logic
Source: Abe Cofnas and Sridhar Iyer

weapons of reconnaissance and detection that allow the trader to identify threats to the profits he has gained. Why is this important as a tool
for improving trading exits and capturing more profits? The answer is
that by setting Renko bricks to a small or microlevel price increment, if
a pattern results, even at a very small increment, this pattern will enable
the earliest possible detection of a change in sentiment. The trader
needs to detect such changes so that he can capture and protect the
profits he has achieved. In currency trading, for example, a few seconds
can be enough to wipe out all of the pips gained, and the price can easily reverse into negative territory. Using Renko charts, the trader gains

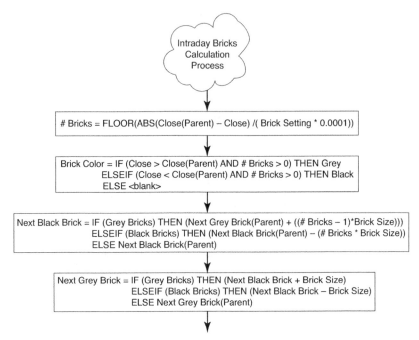

Figure 8.2 Renko Construction Supplemental Logic
Source: Abe Cofnas and Sridhar Iyer

the ability to quantify the persistence of sentiment. If bullish sentiment is prevailing, the trader will be able to detect a bullish pattern even at the micro level. Depending on the trading instrument, we will see that the micro level of trading can be one minute or less. When using Renko charts, bullish sentiment is easily recognizable as a sequence of bullish (green, grey, or white) bricks. If bearish sentiment is prevailing, a descending series of bearish bricks, easily recognized by a black or red color, will appear. Detecting a change in the persistence of sentiment is the key to getting out before profits disappear.

We can see in **Figure 8.3** the dominance of bullish sentiment. The bricks move upwards nearly uninterruptedly in an obvious bullish pattern. Now, let's take a closer look. We can see that the bullish run-up has intermittent interruptions with bricks reversing down. The first reversal was a one-brick reversal, followed by a four-brick reversal, a two-brick reversal, and a one-brick reversal. Finally, we see a five-brick reversal.

RENKO CHARTS CONSTRUCTION LOGIC

Renko charts construction uses the following series of formulae:

Brick Size

Brick size in basis points * 0.0001

Number of Bricks

FLOOR(ABS(Close Price – Parent Close Price)/(Brick Size))

Brick Color

IF (Close Price GREATER THAN Parent Close Price AND #Bricks GREATER THAN 0) THEN Grey

ELSE IF (Close Price LESS THAN Parent Close Price AND #Bricks GREATER THAN 0) Then Black

ELSE <no color>

Next Black Brick

IF (Current Layout are Grey Bricks) THEN

Next Grey Brick position recorded for the Parent Close Price + ((#Bricks – 1) * Brick Size)

ELSE IF (Current Layout are Black Bricks) THEN

Next Black Brick position recorded for the Parent Close Price – (#Bricks * Brick Size)

ELSE

Next Black Brick position recorded for the Parent Close Price

Next Grey Brick

IF (Current Layout are Grey Bricks) THEN

Next Black Brick + Brick Size

ELSE IF (Current Layout are Black Bricks) THEN

Next Black Brick – Brick Size

ELSE Next Grey Brick position recorded for the Parent Close Price

User Input:

Accept user input or set default Brick Size.

Base Construction Logic:

1. Read Base Date and Base Close Price.
2. Read Next Date and Next Close Price.
3. Calculate Brick Size.

(continued)

Renko Charts Construction Logic (*continued*)

Iterative Construction Logic:

1. Read Date and Close Price.
2. Calculate Number of Bricks.
3. Calculate Brick Color.
4. Lay out the bricks.
5. Calculate position of the Next Black Brick.
6. Calculate position of the Next Grey Brick.
7. Return to step 1 of the Iterative Construction Logic.

The challenge is to determine what level of reversal provides the trigger to get out of a position. Should the trader get out at the immediate appearance of Renko bricks of a reverse color? The answer to this question can be significant in many ways. First, the answer will reveal the psychological disposition of the trader. A very skittish

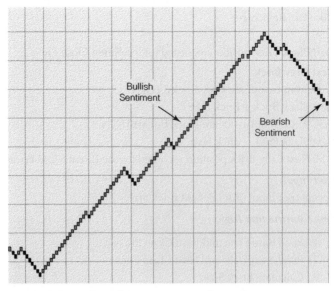

Figure 8.3 Renko Chart Showing Dominant Bullish Sentiment
Source: Chart copyright www.ProRealTime.com

trader will get out on the first appearance of a brick of reverse color. A one- or two-brick reversal is natural and is part of how the price action vibrates. Three bricks reversing would be the threshold at which the trader who wants to protect profits would lighten up or get out. Therefore, as shown on the chart in **Figure 8.4**, the trader would exit half of the position on the appearance of four bricks, and the rest on the appearance of five bricks. These rules make sense when the context is intrahour and intraday trading and the trader is looking for high-frequency moves that will let him capture small amounts.

These Renko exit rules provide a nearly zero tolerance for having a profit turn into a loss. Once a position becomes profitable, the concept is never to allow the position to turn into a loss. It doesn't matter if the original limit or target is much further away. The original target reflects a hypothesis that market conditions anticipated by the trader will be fulfilled. In contrast, Renko chart-based trading is a pure reaction strategy for profit protection. This strategy follows a simple dictum: *Never let a profit turn into a loss.*

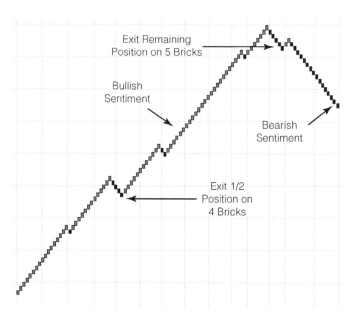

Figure 8.4 Exit Strategies Using Renko Block Reversal Levels
Source: Chart copyright www.ProRealTime.com

Tactical Trading Rules for Renko Charts

Let's summarize some generic rules for the use of Renko charts in trading. First, we have the setting size. Since Renko charts' main use is for determining when a reversal is a threat, the setting size needs to be the smallest level at which the detection of a change in sentiment is meaningful. One percent can be a good starting level for brick sizes. It provides a small enough time frame to capture sentiment changes and a big enough time frame to be robust and not generate unnecessary noise. While setting size is a judgment call, the idea is to get to a size that is as small as is feasible.

A second factor that affects the setting size is targeted risk level. For example, if a trader has an average risk of sixty points, a brick size of ten points will mean that when a position turns to a loss, three bricks would be equivalent to one half of the sixty-point *risk*. A setting of five points would mean that three bricks would be alerting the trader that 25 percent of the risk level has been reached. In this way, we can use setting size in Renko charts as a risk alert.

The next important parameter is the chart interval. The main idea, once again, is to sample the price movement at a high frequency. Therefore, the trader should log into one-minute candle charts and convert them to Renko charts. Of course, there is no harm in comparing Renko chart movements from three time frames. Levels of 89 ticks, 1 minute, and 3 minutes will allow a range of granularity in evaluating sentiment changes.

A third parameter is the number of bricks needed to trigger an exit. Three bricks should be the standard for legging out of a position, but only after the trader has achieved profits. For example, if a currency trade has generated 9 pips in profits, three Renko chart bricks of a reverse color would trigger an exit. The result may be the capture of some small profit, but it would almost always result in prevention of a loss. While there is no general rule for how profitable a position should be to implement a Renko charts exit, a good time to begin is when the trade has entered 30 percent of the target profits. With this rule, one can leg out of one-third or one-half of the position, protect the profits gained, and still be able to participate in a larger profit if the sentiment reverses and continues in the desired direction. Legging out with Renko charts also provides a psychological level of comfort. Most traders use their gut instincts to exit a position when it is profitable, even though Renko chart bricks do not show any reversals and may not be indicating any reason to get out. When such instincts prevail, compromise with the rule, get out of half of the position, and let the Renko chart procedures apply to the other half.

Key Components of a Renko Charts Trade

Let's summarize the key steps in Renko charts trading.

Step 1: Set brick size at 1 percent of the price movement or one-third of average stop-loss. The brick size should be small enough to allow a detection of a stable pattern, and should align with the trader's goals. One- and two-brick sequences (**Figures 8.5** and **8.6**) are the result of the lack of dominance of either bullish or bearish sentiment. A choppy pattern would show a frequent alternation of one- and two-brick sequences.

A trader with an average target of five dollars could set the brick size to ten cents. This would be a reasonable Renko charts size: not too big and not too small. If the stop loss target were fifty cents, a brick size of five cents would be more acceptable. The trader following the rule of three would get out at a fifteen-cent loss.

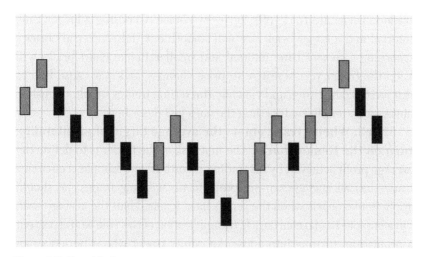

Figure 8.5 Unstable Pattern
Source: Chart copyright www.ProRealTime.com

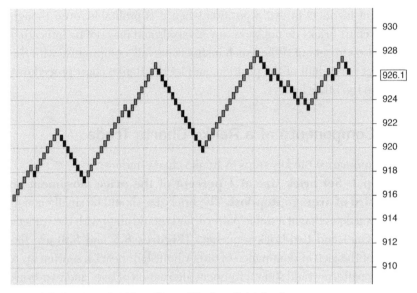

Figure 8.6 One-Hour Gold Spot Chart, Fifty-Cent Brick Setting

Source: Chart copyright www.ProRealTime.com

Step 2: Select chart time interval; use three time intervals.
The best approach to applying Renko charting after profits are emerging is to set the time interval to the lowest possible one that generates a stable Renko chart pattern. This interval may vary with the instrument traded. There are trade-offs for every choice. Choosing a longer time interval and a larger brick size will smooth out "false reversal" bricks. Choosing a shorter time interval and smaller Renko chart bricks will keep the trader very sensitive to price changes, and may cause him to exit too quickly. Using, and viewing, three time frames simultaneously is always a better alternative than the ones just described.

Step 3: When a trade enters the average target of profitability, turn on the Renko charts. The first task of the trader is to define the average profit achieved by his trading record. If, for example, a currency trader has an average ten-pip profit in his winning trades, he should apply Renko charts when the profits have reached half the average goal. On a one-pip Renko chart brick, the application of this rule would prevent a profit from turning into a loss. An equity trader who experiences an average profit of twenty cents on a stock and a stop-loss of fifteen cents would set the Renko charts brick size to five cents.

Fear and Renko

Whether traders are bullish or bearish, once they are in a position, they have one fear in common: that an opposite sentiment is rising. In many ways, this concept of detection of the level of sentiment against the trader is similar to obtaining a medical diagnosis about infection levels. If a trader were in a selling mode, being infected with bullish units of sentiment would be a concern. Similarly, a trader who is in a buying mode would want to see no increase in the units of selling sentiment. In effect, Renko chart bricks are units of infection. Bullish sentiment is an infection of the bearish position, and vice versa. In Renko charting, the enemy of the bullish trader is the appearance of black or red Renko chart bricks. The enemy of the bearish trader is the appearance of gray, green, or white Renko charts bricks. The trader is always looking for signs of an increase in the sentiment against his intended direction. The bullish trader is afraid that, like an infection, any increase in the levels of red or black bricks will eat away at his profits. That adversarial view makes him sensitive to not letting the profits turn into a loss.

Step 1: Renko Chart Setting Sizes and Time Intervals

The exact Renko charts brick size and time interval that a trader will settle on will vary with the strategy and style of the trader. The process for deciding on the brick size should not be arbitrary, but instead should be the outcome of a sensitivity analysis. One needs to test what changes in settings will do to the resulting brick patterns. The key question is whether the resulting Renko brick pattern is more or less stable than the prior one.

Let's look at some patterns for different trading markets.

Gold and Renko Chart Variations

Let's compare two gold spot charts. Each has a period of one hour. The first chart (**Figure 8.6**) has a setting of fifty cents for the Renko brick size. The second chart (**Figure 8.7**) has a setting of one dollar. The setting of fifty cents shows three appearances of a black brick down reversal, and three appearances of a one-brick up reversal. In contrast, notice that the gold spot chart with the one-dollar setting shows no appearance

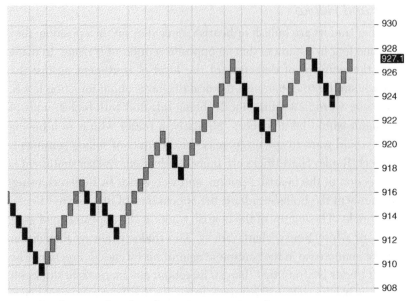

Figure 8.7 One-Hour Gold Spot Chart, One-Dollar Brick Setting
Source: Chart copyright www.ProRealTime.com

of a vibrating brick. This leads to the question of which setting is better. The one-dollar setting allows longer trade duration because there is no technical reason to get out. A smaller setting promotes capturing profits earlier. One cannot come to a clear conclusion about setting size without understanding the total performance metrics of the trader.

Crude Oil and Renko Chart Variations

We compared a crude oil one-hour chart with a brick size of fifty cents **(Figure 8.8)** against a crude oil ten-minute chart with a brick size of twenty-five cents **(Figure 8.9)**. In this example, we have reduced the time interval as well as the brick size. The result is greater ability to detect a change in the sentiment. The smaller brick size enabled the trader to detect a fifty-cent pullback and the beginning of a sideways market. We can see this at the most extreme right edge. For the trader looking to capture profits, this kind of pattern would be an alert. Still, the one-minute crude oil chart with a setting of ten cents **(Figure 8.10)** provides the greatest granularity. The trader can see the choppiness in the sentiment.

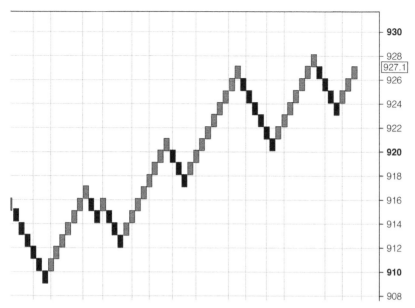

Figure 8.8 U.S. Crude Oil, June 2009: Renko Block 0.50, One-Hour Interval
Source: Chart copyright www.ProRealTime.com

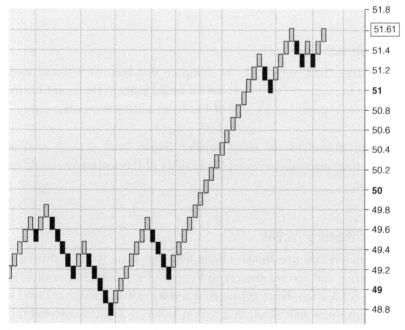

Figure 8.9 U.S. Crude Oil, June 2009: Renko Block 0.25, Ten-Minute Interval
Source: Chart copyright www.ProRealTime.com

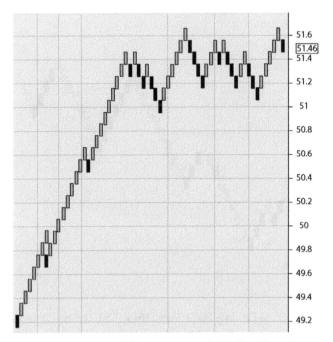

Figure 8.10 U.S. Crude Oil, June 2009: Renko Block 0.10, One-Minute Interval

Source: Chart copyright www.ProRealTime.com

Dow Jones Cash

In **Figures 8.11** and **8.12**, we compare one-hour Dow Jones cash against a five-minute interval. Here we see a 1 percent Renko setting for the one-hour period and a 1/10 of 1 percent setting for the five-minute period.

Again, the virtue of using smaller Renko brick size as well as smaller time intervals to reveal the tonality of the sentiment should be apparent.

U.S. Treasury Notes

Bond traders can use Renko charts with the same level of precision as currency and futures traders to leg out of a profitable position. In **Figure 8.13**, a one-hour, 0.1 percent setting in T-notes showed twelve consecutive new low closes in a row. A seller of T-notes enjoying this downward move and using a rule of getting out at three brick reversals would get out when three reversals occur. A setting of one hour and ten

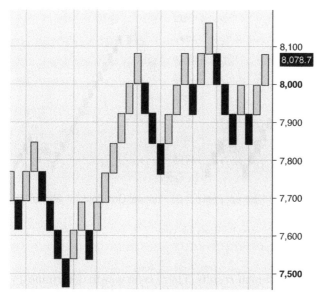

Figures 8.11 Dow Jones Cash: Renko 1%, Interval One Hour
Source: Chart copyright www.ProRealTime.com

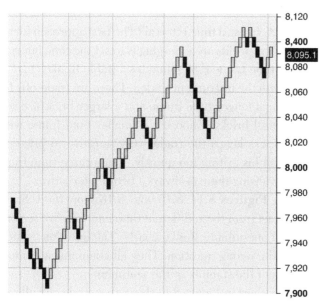

Figure 8.12 Dow Jones Cash: Renko 0.001%, Interval Five Minutes
Source: Chart copyright www.ProRealTime.com

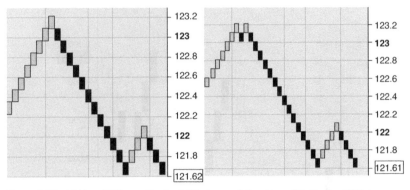

Figure 8.13 10-Year T-Notes: Renko 0.01, Interval One Hour (L); Renko 10 Points, Interval One Hour

Source: Chart copyright www.ProRealTime.com

points provided similar results. There is no way to determine an optimal setting in advance. Traders need to adjust the settings based on their own preferences.

Step 2: Select Chart Time Interval: Use Three Time Intervals

How can we best choose a time interval? The best approach for applying Renko charts when profits are emerging is to set the time interval to the lowest possible time frame that generates a stable Renko chart pattern. This may vary with the instrument traded. There are trade-offs for every choice. Choosing a longer time frame and a larger brick size smoothes out "false" reversal bricks. Choosing a smaller time frame with small Renko charts bricks keeps the trader very sensitive to price changes, and may result in his exiting too quickly. Using three time frames and simultaneously viewing them is always a better alternative.

For example, **Figures 8.14**, **8.15**, and **8.16** show the U.S. crude oil June 2009 contract from three different time intervals. We see one-hour, ten-minute, and one-minute Renko charts. The question "which is the best chart?" is the wrong question. They all communicate information to the trader about the stability of the sentiment.

The one-hour chart in Figure 8.14 shows that crude oil bull sentiment was, from the perspective of one hour, able to sustain six consecutive new closes above fifty cents. More revealing is the Renko chart with a

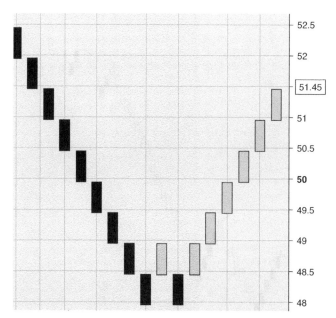

Figure 8.14 U.S. Crude Oil: Renko Block 0.50, Interval One Hour

Source: Chart copyright www.ProRealTime.com

ten-minute, twenty-five cent setting (Figure 8.15). The adjustment down of the setting provides an enhanced confirmation of the bull sentiment. The market allowed this crude to achieve seventeen consecutive new twenty-five cent moves without a reversal. A trader using a criterion of getting out after three reversals down in Renko chart bricks would be staying in all the way.

The one-minute chart, with a further adjustment down of ten cents a brick, shows more choppiness when the price went to 51.4. If the trader were already in profits, using a one-minute Renko chart with a ten-cent setting would cause him to lighten up.

Step 3: When a Trade Enters the Average Target of Profitability, Turn On the Renko Charts

Many traders forget to keep track of their total record of performance. They focus on the cash value of their account as the measure of success. This is an oversight because it makes it difficult for the trader to diagnose his trading weaknesses correctly. Among the first tasks of the trader is

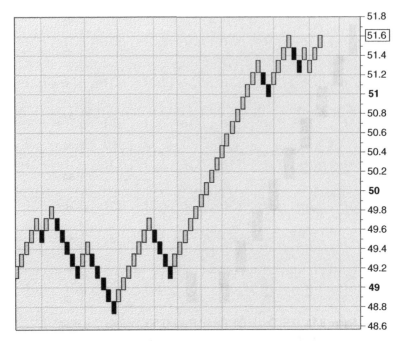

Figure 8.15 U.S. Crude Oil: Renko Block .25, Interval Ten Minutes
Source: Chart copyright www.ProRealTime.com

to define the average profit achieved in his trading record. If, for example, a currency trader has on the average a ten-pip profit in his winning trades, he should apply Renko charts when the profits have reached half the average goal. On a one-pip Renko chart brick, the application of this rule would prevent a profit from turning into a loss. An equity trader experiencing an average profit of 20 cents on a stock using a stop-loss of 15 cents would set the Renko charts brick size to .05 cents.

Time and Bricks

The Silent Doji

When trying Renko charts, many traders will watch the charts and see that nothing seems to be happening. The Renko chart bricks have not moved. Often, when seeing this, the trader believes something is wrong. This is not an error in the feed. It represents hesitation. The sentiment is not able to register a change. We can call this pause in the Renko charts bricks a *silent Doji*. The trader, upon sensing the silence, should

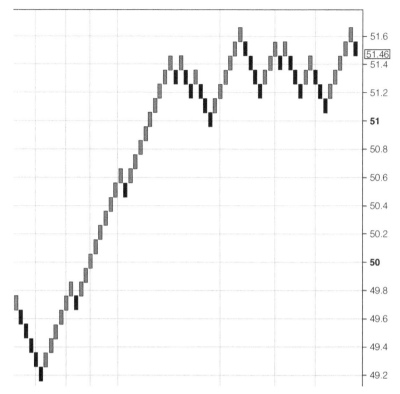

Figure 8.16 U.S. Crude Oil: Renko Block 0.10, Interval One Minute
Source: Chart copyright www.ProRealTime.com

be on alert that a movement could occur at any second. However, a silent Doji does not have to be silent at all. Programmers can build in an alarm that scans the duration of no movement in the Renko chart bricks and sets off an alarm alerting the trader.

Bricks per Minute or Bricks per Tick

A useful observation to quantify the change in sentiment is the measure of bricks per minute. Platforms showing Renko should provide this data. Since Renko charts only add or subtract another brick when the price has closed with the specified setting distance, Renko charts provide a very good visual track of sentiment momentum. Logically, the faster bricks are added to the charts, the stronger the momentum. A shift in bricks per minute is a leading indicator of momentum changes in the

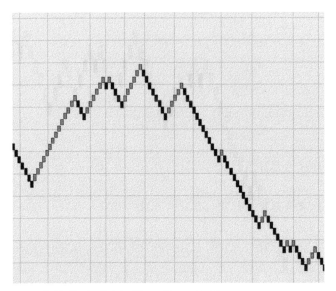

Figure 8.17 Renko Bricks Show Change in Momentum

Source: Chart copyright www.ProRealTime.com

sentiment. Such a change in momentum in Renko bricks is apparent in the chart in **Figure 8.17**.

In some markets, the trader can go to an even smaller setting, such as ticks. *Ticks* are the actual trades going through the platform, and provide an accurate surrogate for volume. Settings of 50 and 89 ticks should be compared to a setting of one minute. If the tick settings result in very choppy Renko bricks, the trader should adjust upward to smooth out the choppiness. Often, even at tick levels, we can detect patterns showing the dominance of bullish or bearish sentiment.

Renko Charts and Economic Data Release Trading

Most of the markets react to economic data releases, and price action around those releases is well known. The market hesitates before a data release and forms a sideways pattern. Prior to the release, there is a period of price movement testing support or resistance. This occurs approximately five to ten minutes before the data release, as traders try to gain positions in anticipation of the news. The economic data release triggers a reaction if the data reports results that surprise the market.

The reaction is similar to a reaction–diffusion chemical process; it's like a drop of acidic economic data release entering a "base" of hesitation! Economic data releases are perhaps the most important scheduled event that moves the markets. Yet it is conventional wisdom to avoid trading these economic data releases and wait for the market's reaction. Renko charts provide a highly precise ability to trade economic data releases in several ways.

Consider the example of the surprise Swiss Central Bank intervention on March 12, 2009. The intervention caused a virtual price shock wave with a 400-pip move in the USDCHF currency pair. Since it was not a scheduled event nor a calendar release, the traders could not anticipate playing the move from its onset. We can see the magnitude of the move from both a day candle perspective (**Figure 8.18a**) and the one-minute perspective (**Figure 8.18b**).

Let's see what happens when we use Renko charts (**Figure 8.19**). The trader could jump into the direction and stay in it until the Renko chart bricks reversed. Alternatively, watching Renko charts showed when to reenter the position: after a Renko chart high had been established and then taken out again after a retracement down. This is a case where we can use Renko charts *to enter* a position. With a one-minute Renko chart, it was easier to detect pattern changes, and therefore changes in sentiment, even though they occurred in the middle of the action. Renko charts provide a superior ability to map momentum at micro levels in high-frequency situations, such as in the immediate time frame of economic data releases.

Renko Charts and Economic Data Releases: Trading Strategy Variations

The best way to use Renko charts for trading economic data releases is to use Renko charts *after* one puts on a position, no matter what kind of entry criteria one uses. Let's review some of the common variations for trading the economic data release, and then apply Renko charts.

➤ **Anticipating a position:** In this strategy, the trader selects an anticipated direction. If the economic data release reaction is agreeable, the position has moved into profitability instantly. The question is, how and when to get out?

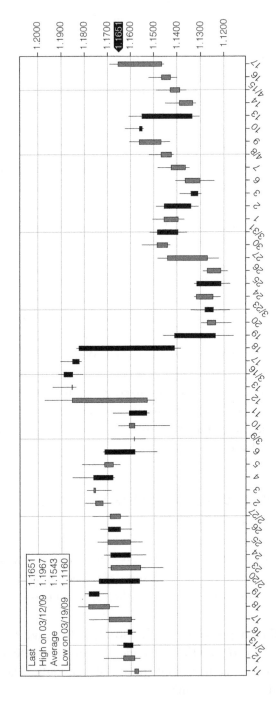

Figure 8.18a Swiss Franc, Day Candlestick Chart, March 11–May 15, 2009

Source: Chart copyright www.ProRealTime.com

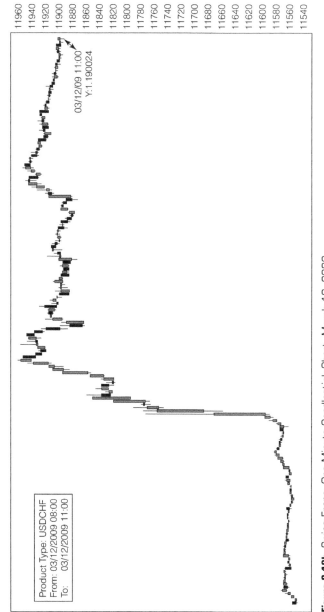

Figure 8.18b Swiss Franc, One-Minute-Candlestick Chart, March 12, 2009

Source: Chart copyright www.ProRealTime.com

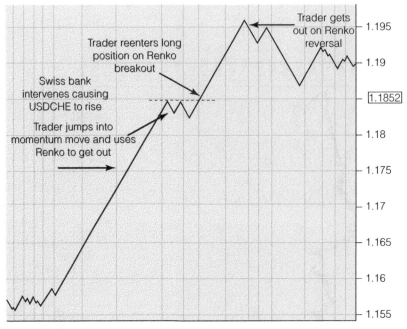

Figure 8.19 Swiss Franc, One-Minute Renko Chart, March 12, 2009

➤ **Hedging the news:** In this strategy, the trader does not have an anticipated direction but plays both sides by putting on a buy and a sell at the same time. When the economic data release breaks, the trader gets out of the losing side and rides the winner. The question, again, is determining when to exit the winning position.

➤ **Post–economic data release retracement:** In this strategy, the trader waits for the economic data release, and then waits for the price to complete its reaction. The trader enters after the reaction is complete and uses Fibonacci resistance-based entry strategies. Once again, after entry, how long should the trader hold on to the profitable position?

In every variation of an economic release trading strategy, Renko charts provide a degree of precision for exiting. At the moment of an economic data release, the sentiment energy is at a maximum. It is a period of hypertrading, and technical indicators will not work effectively because they lag the action. Renko charts are most effective because they enable the trader to visualize whether there is persistence of sentiment in the direction of the break, thereby providing unprecedented accuracy.

Using Renko Charts to Enter Positions

We have discussed the main use of Renko charts: as an exit tool for the trader, particularly once he has achieved a profitable position. There are three occasions where Renko charts can be used as an entry tool. The first is upon the appearance of a parabolic curve; the second is with Fibonacci resistance lines/pivot point retracements; and the third is with Bollinger bands.

Renko Charts and Parabolic Curves

Parabolic curves, when they appear, are signatures of unstable sentiment. Surging behavior, often in response to economic data releases, culminates in a peak and then reverses. Trading parabolic curves is dangerous because it is difficult to determine when the momentum is over. There is great risk of a whipsaw. Once again, Renko charts help out by enabling traders to quantify when there is a detectable and meaningful change in sentiment. The charts in **Figures 8.20** and **8.21** show the same parabolic curve in a candle pattern and a Renko chart pattern. The Renko chart is a clearer chart for shaping a trading strategy. Once the candlestick chart shows that a parabolic curve is forming, the trader can move to the Renko chart version, enter a market order, and stay in the position until there is a reversal of three Renko chart bricks. In cases where the trader has noted a parabolic curve but is looking to fade the position, he will wait for a reversal in the Renko chart bricks and then enter the action.

The reason Renko charting works well here is that is it a coincident indicator. Every Renko chart brick that appears represents a successful survival of an increment of sentiment. In Renko chart trading, the battle between bulls and bears is a battle of colored bricks. Armed with Renko Charts the trader can use Renko Charts after entering a momentum trade and watch the brick movement. As long as the preferred-color bricks keep moving in the intended direction, the trade will be in good shape. The key factor will be the brick size. Once again, one must calibrate it to achieve a balance of factors. Too small a brick size will result

Figure 8.20 Candlestick Chart with Parabolic Curve

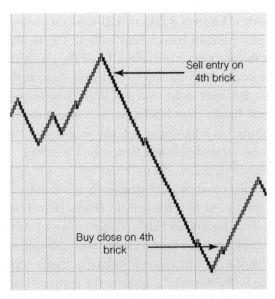

Figure 8.21 Renko Chart Entry/Exit Strategy with Parabolic Curve

in choppy patterns and false signals. Too large a brick size will result in lagging indicators.

Renko Charts and Fibonacci Resistance Lines

A powerful method to increase confirmation of price sentiment changes is to overlay Renko charts with Fibonacci resistance lines. In **Figure 8.22**, we can see that the Renko chart bricks formed a high-to-low wave and then made several attempts to retrace back to the origin. A trader may want to trade the retracement attempt and use Renko chart bricks as a guide. Where is the best entry point? In these scenarios, if Renko chart bricks are moving through a key Fibonacci resistance line ratio such as 61.8, a buy setup is in effect.

Renko Charts and Bollinger Bands

An example of how Renko charts can be used with Bollinger bands is when a trader is looking for an entry setup. A common entry setup using candlesticks and Bollinger bands occurs when the candle is sliding

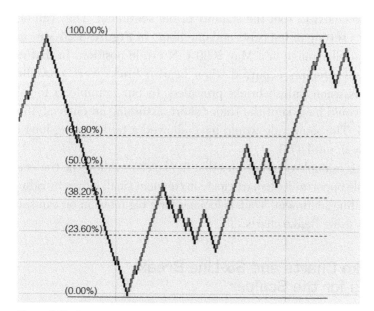

Figure 8.22 Enter on Renko Break of 61.8% Line
Source: Chart copyright www.ProRealTime.com

down the band and shows no sign of retracing back up. The trader would have to play a guessing game as to what would be the entry trigger. The Renko chart pattern helps out. In the EURUSD one-minute chart in **Figure 8.23**, Renko chart bricks had a breakdown of support at the same time that the candlestick on the five-minute chart was sliding down the Bollinger band. This acts as a confirmation of entry.

Renko Charts in Multiple Markets

Gold

In **Figure 8.24**, we see three Renko chart time frames: five minutes, one minute, and tick by tick. The gold commodity or spot trader can see support in all three charts at 925.50. However, the one-minute chart shows a fast-paced sentiment in selling off: it took twelve minutes to complete ten bricks up, versus six bricks in two minutes. The sentiment speed was 1.2 bricks per minute, versus three bricks per minute.

Crude Oil

Traders of crude oil can gain an insight into intraday trading by using Renko charts to spot the stability of the sentiment. They can do this using a setting of ten cents and one hour. In **Figure 8.25**, we can see a five-dollar range in a May 2009 U.S. crude position. In that range, reversal attempts occurred when bearish bricks were prevailing as well as when bullish bricks prevailed. In our example, a four-brick rule would have kept the trader short, assuming an entry at 48.45 to 44.88. The same rule would have allowed a trader going long at 45 to stay in until 47.3.

This example demonstrates that Renko charts allow the trader a reasonable opportunity to participate in frequent small moves by riding the prevailing sentiment. Traders looking for a big move in oil can surf the waves using Renko charts.

Renko Charts and Six-Line Break: Tools for the Scalper

What happens when we compare Renko charts and six-line price break charts for entry purposes?

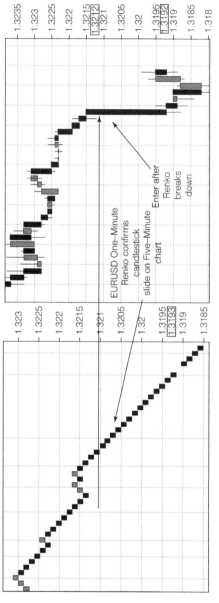

Figure 8.23 Entry Setup Using Candlesticks and Bollinger Bands

Source: Chart copyright www.ProRealTime.com

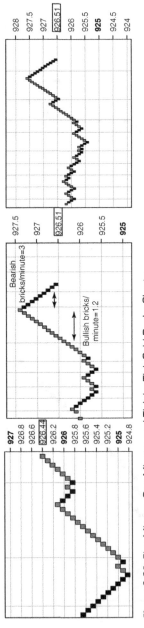

Figure 8.24 Five-Minute, One-Minute, and Tick-by-Tick Gold Renko Charts

Source: Chart copyright www.ProRealTime.com

134

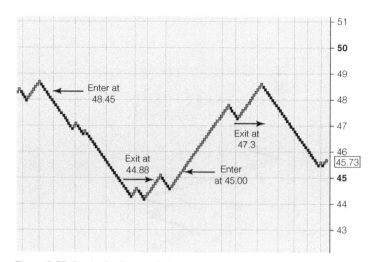

Figure 8.25 Renko Surfing the Waves
Source: Chart copyright www.ProRealTime.com

Figure 8.26 is a gold one-minute chart with Renko chart and six-line price break chart settings. The six-line price break chart showed a projected reversal point on April 23 at 12:23 of 894.24. Following this projection, the trader would enter a buy stop order just beyond that point to give the price some room to move. From a Renko charts perspective, the Renko chart's white bricks reached a peak of 893.66 on April 23 at 14:35. Gold broke through at 14:57 and continued to 898.92. Using both price break charts and Renko charts, we can see that each contributed differently but effectively. Price break charts gave an earlier projection of an upward break. Renko charts broke out of the resistance that had formed two hours later. Tactically, the trader could use both.

EURJPY

Envision a scalper who likes to jump into a position and get out as soon as possible. In **Figure 8.27**, the combination of Renko bricks and six-line breaks works well to confirm the state of the momentum. We can see that the Renko sequence of down bricks coincided with the price break reversal.

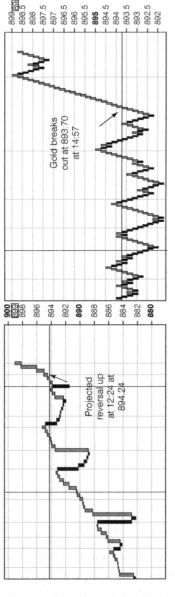

Figure 8.26 Gold One-Minute Chart: Renko and Six-Line Price Break Settings

Source: Chart copyright www.ProRealTime.com

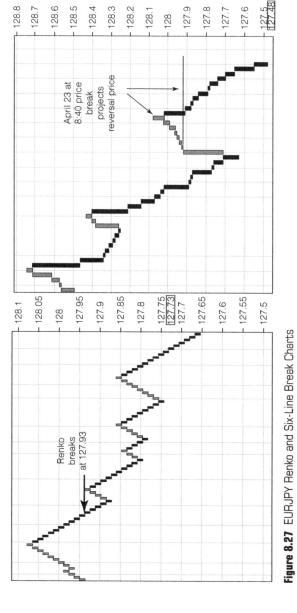

Figure 8.27 EURJPY Renko and Six-Line Break Charts

Source: Chart copyright www.ProRealTime.com

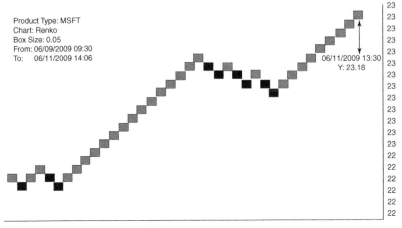

Product Type: MSFT
Chart: Renko
Box Size: 0.05
From: 06/09/2009 09:30
To: 06/11/2009 14:06

06/11/2009 13:30
Y: 23.18

Figure 8.28 Renko Strategy: MSFT
Source: Abe Cofnas and Sridhar Iyer

Renko Bricks at the Tick Level

Can we use Renko bricks at the tick level? In traditional charting, we usually get a lot of noise at this level. The logic of Renko charts is that if a pattern appears, it has an origin at the smallest intervals. We would expect tick levels to show patterns that can inform the trader of sentiment changes.

What is remarkable about Renko brick charting is its ability to smooth out the noise and clearly demonstrate that a pattern exists even at the tick level. In **Figure 8.28**, we see a Microsoft Renko chart using tick data. The Renko brick size is 0.5 percent. Using the three-brick rule, a trader buying at 22 right after a break in the sideways action would have stayed in the position and been able to withstand the slight decline because there were never three bricks in a row down.

A trader using Renko strategy for Google, with a box size of 0.05 percent, could have captured nearly a six-dollar move, as there was no evidence of bullish sentiment (**Figure 8.29**).

Renko and Volume

Let's take a look at a Renko brick formation using tick-level data and volume. In **Figure 8.30**, we see Renko ticks with volume on Caterpillar. The trader should look for a spike in the volume and then see if it is associated with the beginning of a reversal lock. Additionally, a spike in

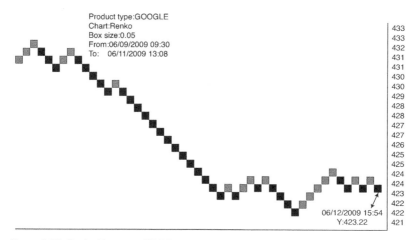

Figure 8.29 Renko Strategy: GOOG

Source: Abe Cofnas and Sridhar Iyer

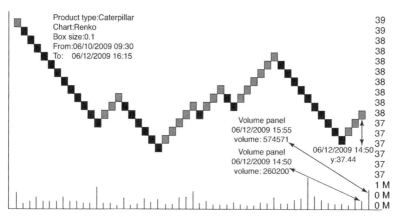

Figure 8.30 Renko Ticks with Volume: CAT

Source: Abe Cofnas and Sridhar Iyer

the middle of a Renko brick series would indicate a strong propensity to continue in that direction.

Chapter Note

1. Eugen Santos Jr. and Qunhua Zhao, "Adversarial Models for Opponent Intent Inferencing," from *Adversarial Reasoning—Computational Approaches to Reading the Opponent's Mind,* edited by Alexander Kott and William M McEneaney (Chapman & Hall/CRC), page 1.

CHAPTER 9

Kagi Charts
Waiting for the Turn
of Sentiment

THE AIM OF this chapter is to provide an understanding of Kagi charting, its basic concepts, and its key applications in trading.

Kagi Chart Basics

Kagi means "key" in Japanese, and the idea behind using Kagi charts is to use them as a key to detecting turns in sentiment more effectively. The best way for a trader to use Kagi charts, like Renko charts, is after the trader has decided upon the direction of the next trade. Once the trader makes a directional decision, the challenge is to find the optimal entry point. Of course, there is controversy as to what is optimal. Generally, there is no best place to enter a trade, but there are many combinations of conditions that result in an optimal setup. Our focus here is on how the trader can use Kagi as an entry trigger. A major reason to use Kagi for entering a trade is that Kagi pinpoints when the sentiment has turned. This is what Kagi charts are all about. Kagi charts are very effective with regard to displaying sentiment changes.

Let's start by defining the main characteristics of the Kagi chart that provide tools for analysis.

Yin and Yang: These are the Kagi chart lines. They alternate between being thin and thick. *Yin* is the name associated with the sentiment being bearish and favoring selling. When *Yang* lines emerge, buying sentiment has taken over. Yang lines are thicker than Yin lines. In some charts the differences between the lines are visualized as colors: the Yang lines are gray or green and the Yin lines are red or black.

Shoulders. When the line changes from thin to thick, a Kagi *shoulder* is formed, generating a down reversal.

Kagi waistlines. *Waistlines* are the opposite of shoulders, and occur when the line changes from thick to thin, generating an up reversal.

Turning—the main Kagi chart event. The key to understanding Kagi charts is the relationship between Yin and Yang. The benefit of Kagi charts is that they show the nature of the existing balance of sentiment more clearly for some traders. The key Kagi chart visual that becomes a signal is the change from Yin to Yang or Yang to Yin **(Figure 9.1)**.

Reversal amount. *Reversal amount* is the amount that, if equaled or exceeded by the price, will cause a turn. The reversal amount can be either a fixed amount or a percentage. A percentage is much more scalable. There is no consensus on a setting for the turnaround; the trader has to do a balancing act. Reversal amounts must be small enough to generate reliable signals of a shift in sentiment. On the other hand, too large a setting would miss intraday signals and be useful mostly to long-term traders. Reversal amounts therefore need to be a function of trading strategy. Short-term scalpers will want smaller reversal thresholds than longer-term swing or position traders. However, the subjective nature of the turnaround settings is really a result of neglect among traders. When integrated with other data sets such as three–price break charts, the turnaround amount for Kagi charts should be the setting that results

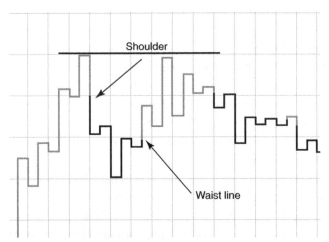

Figure 9.1 Turning—The Main Kagi Chart Event
Source: Chart copyright www.ProRealTime.com

in a maximum correlation between projected price break chart and Kagi chart turnarounds.

Reversal location. A key criterion for the trader is the *reversal location*. Is the reversal at a key Fibonacci resistance line or other technical parameter? Another projected reversal point can be the middle of a long Yin or Yang line.

Price close. Kagi charts lines use price close only for calibrating the charts.

The following is the construction logic for Kagi charts. It follows the rules set forth in *Beyond Candlesticks: New Japanese Charting Techniques Revealed* (Nison, Wiley). Flowcharts illustrating Kagi chart construction logic are found in **Figures 9.2** and **9.3**.

Kagi Chart Construction Logic

User Input:
Accept user input or set default values for the following:

- Percentage Reversal Price Amount;
- Distance above Shoulder (High) in basis points;
- Distance below Kagi Waist (Low) in basis points.

Base Construction Logic:

1. Read Base Date and Base Close Price.
2. Set Line Tip Price to Base Close Price.
3. Compute Turnaround Price Decisions at Line Tip as follows:
   a. Reversal Amount = (Line Tip Price) * (Fixed Percentage Reversal Amount) / 100
   b. Turnaround Price Decision (Low Point) = Line Tip Price − Reversal Amount
   c. Turnaround Price Decision (High Point) = Line Tip Price + Reversal Amount
4. Read (Next) Date, (Next) Close price.
5. If (Next) Close Price drops less than the Turnaround Low Price Decision Point, then a Yin line is drawn downwards from Line Tip to the (Next) Close Price.

(Continued)

Kagi Chart Construction Logic (*Continued*)

6. If (Next) Close Price is more than the Turnaround High Price Decision Point, then a Yang line is drawn upward from Line Tip to the (Next) Close Price.

7. If the (Next) Close Price falls between Turnaround Price Decision Low/High Points (inclusive) then the first line is not drawn and the (Next) Close Price record is skipped.

8. If first line is drawn, then set the new Line Tip Price to the (Next) Close Price.

9. For the new Line Tip Price, compute the Turnaround Price Decision (Low/High) Points based on formula defined in step 3 of the *Base Construction Logic*.

Iterative Construction Logic:

1. Read Date and Close Price.

2. If no line is drawn yet, then go to step 4 of the *Base Construction Logic*.

3. If Close Price is in trend with the direction of the existing line, then extend the Yin or Yang line up to the Close Price. Go to step 7 of the *Iterative Construction Logic*.

4. If the absolute difference of the existing Line Tip Price and the Close Price is less than the Reversal Amount calculated at the Line Tip, then ignore Close Price and go to step 1 of the *Iterative Construction Logic*.

5. If uptrend and Close Price is lower than the Line Tip Price by the Reversal Amount, then form Kagi Shoulder inflection and continue the existing Yin or Yang downward. Change line from Yang to Yin when Close Price falls under prior Kagi Waist. Go to step 7 of the *Iterative Construction Logic*.

6. If downtrend and Close Price is greater than the Line Tip Price by the Reversal Amount, then form Kagi Waist inflection and continue the existing Yin or Yang upward. Change line from Yin to Yang when Close price goes above prior Shoulder.

7. Set the new Line Tip Price to the Close Price.

8. For the new Line Tip Price, compute the Turnaround Price Decision (Low/High) Points based on formula defined in step 3 of the *Base Construction Logic*.

9. Go to step 1 of the *Iterative Construction Logic*.

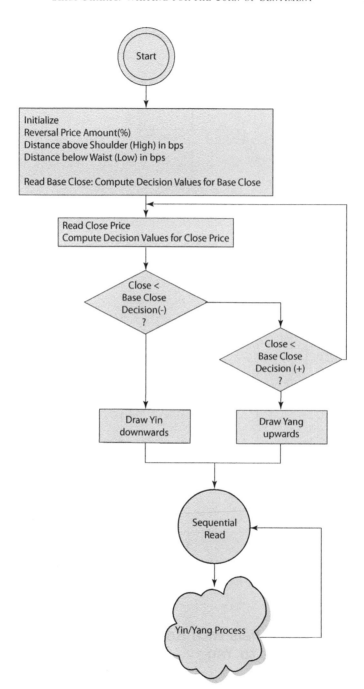

Figure 9.2 Kagi Chart Construction Logic
Source: Abe Cofnas and Sridhar Iyer

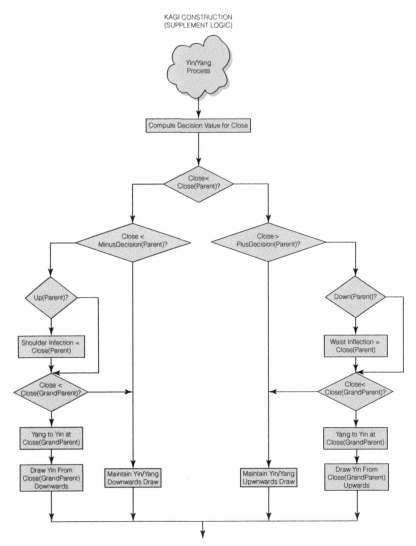

Figure 9.3 Kagi Chart Supplemental Construction Logic
Source: Abe Cofnas and Sridhar Iyer

Buy and Sell Signals with Kagi Charts— When Yin Turns to Yang

There are a variety of buy and sell signals generated by Kagi charts. In this chapter we want to focus only on the main ones. First, we shall consider the use of a trend line on the Kagi charts chart. By applying a trend line to a Kagi chart, the trader can detect whether a Kagi chart is in a buying or selling zone or whether the price is approaching these lines. It is important to note that when Kagi charts appear stable, the pattern confirms the presence of a trend continuation, and this offers a visual level of confirmation.

One way a Kagi-based signal is generated is at the break of a trend line. This is depicted in **Figure 9.4**. We see a line connecting the Kagi shoulders on the left and a line connecting the Kagi waists on the right. This is similar to a candlestick on a downtrend and uptrend line. The lines play the same role in Kagi. If the Kagi chart penetrates the line, it is a break of the trend.

When the Yin turns to the Yang or the Yang turns to the Yin, the trader has a signal. The challenge is whether to take the signal or seek other forms of confirmation. One important confirmation is if the Yin-to-Yang or Yang-to-Yin change is at a 50 percent center line. This would indicate an impending shift in the balance between bulls and bears. In the chart below we see a Kagi Yin to Yang turn coinciding with the downtrend line. This generates a buy signal. A sell signal occurs right after it, because two Kagi shoulders are formed and then Yang turns to Yin. Finally, at the most recent (right) side of the chart, we see a Yin turn to a Yang early at the midpoint.

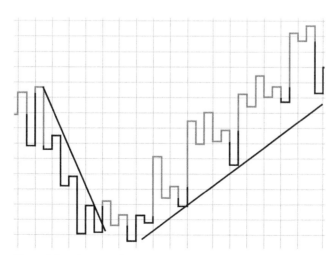

Figure 9.4 A Signal Is Generated at the Break of a Trend Line
Source: Chart copyright www.ProRealTime.com

Kagi Charts: The Keys to the Turn of Sentiment

Kagi charts reveal who is in control and whether there has been a change in the balance of power between buyers and sellers. The length of the Yin or Yang line indicates where the balance or imbalance of sentiment lies. The Kagi chart lines become a continuous sentiment map, and the trader looks for key areas where things may turn (**Figure 9.5**). As we said previously, *Kagi* literally means *key*. As with any charting tool, the goal is to transform the data so it can be visualized with greater clarity than would be possible using bar charts or candlesticks.

Let's compare the Kagi (**Figure 9.6**) and candlestick (**Figure 9.7**) charts of U.S. crude oil for April 2009. Which of the following is clearer? Does the Kagi chart provide clean contours of support and resistance lines? There is much less "noise" in the Kagi charts, whereas the candlestick generates a feeling of noise through the presence of a great number of "tails."

In the spot gold chart in **Figure 9.8**, we can see in the candlestick action that there was a trend line break. What remains vague is a standard for entering the position. Does the trader wait for the price to move further after the break? Let's apply Kagi charting (**Figure 9.9**). Now we can see that there was a Yang-to-Yin change and a Yin-to-Yang

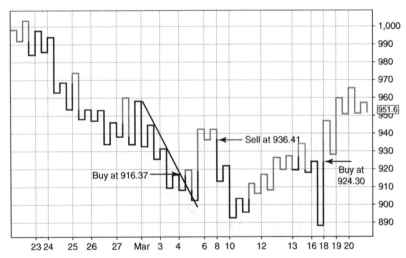

Figure 9.5 Kagi Lines: A Continuous Sentiment Map

Source: Chart copyright www.ProRealTime.com

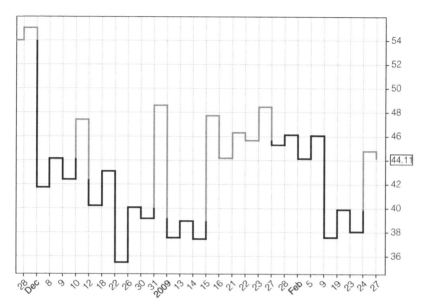

Figure 9.6 Kagi Chart, U.S. Crude Oil, April 2009
Source: Chart copyright www.ProRealTime.com

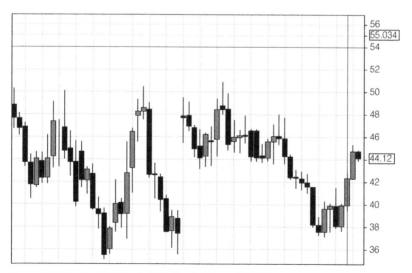

Figure 9.7 Candlestick Chart, U.S. Crude Oil, April 2009
Source: Chart copyright www.ProRealTime.com

conversion. Also notice that a simple shift in the turnaround setting provides enhanced granularity to the trader. The Kagi chart has a 1 percent setting, a setting level that provides good movement without a lot of noise.

Figure 9.8 Spot Gold Candlestick Chart
Source: Chart copyright www.ProRealTime.com

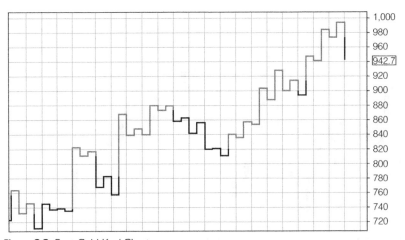

Figure 9.9 Spot Gold Kagi Chart
Source: Chart copyright www.ProRealTime.com

Alternative Settings for Kagi Turnovers

Just as in Renko charting, the trader using Kagi charts can vary the turnaround setting to suit the style of trading. However, a good practice is to view three Kagi charts at the same time, using alternative settings. This will enable the trader to detect the setting that gives the best view of the overall patterns. It is also important to set the Kagi turnover level in relationship to the settings being used for Renko or point and figure charts. The Kagi settings should be slightly different to maximize the value of Kagi projections and provide a slightly different perspective.

Quantifying Kagi Charts

Kagi charts are now relatively obscure in their use among traders. This obscurity is primarily because Kagi charts appear out of character with other price charts. The hieroglyphic quality of the Kagi chart lines makes them hard to quantify, and in, particular deters Western traders from learning them. Perhaps it is also the tendency of people to conform to the norm instead of exploring new areas. Despite this, taking another look at Kagi charts is worthwhile because, as we will see, they have the potential to shed new light on key price landmarks for trading. To date, a primary use of Kagi charts has been limited to scanning the charts for key patterns. This approach works well, because it results in identification of relevant support and resistance lines. However, a risk of simply scanning Kagi charts is the trader's relative unfamiliarity with those charts. A Kagi chart reader can easily misidentify a pattern. For those persons who have good pattern recognition ability, Kagi charts can be effective, but for the vast majority they appear too strange and hieroglyphic in form. In response to these difficulties, we present a better approach to the use of Kagi charts. We first convert the same data generated by Kagi charts into a table of key metrics, which becomes a Kagi charts map of price action. Such a table would automatically pinpoint the key results of applying Kagi chart calculations.

The data fields in a Kagi charts price action table should contain at least the following columns:

➤ Whether a price has closed as a Yin or a Yang
➤ The number of consecutive Yins or Yangs

➤ The Yin/Yang ratio
➤ The moving average of the Yin/Yang ratios
➤ The Yin-to-Yang or Yang-to-Yin price break charts point

These are the categories and information that a trader using Kagi should be able to access or create.

Kagi Versus Candlesticks—Which Is Better?

A useful exercise is to generate and compare a Kagi chart with a candlestick chart to determine where key points converge. Do they both project similar resistance and support lines? Is a Kagi chart turnaround at a Fibonacci resistance lines point? We can gain some useful insights by drawing a comparison between these two chart types. **Figure 9.10** shows a Kagi chart for U.S. Treasury bonds (June 2009) that uses a 10–basis point turnaround and a four-hour time interval. The candlestick version is for the same instrument and the same four-hour interval. First, we can see that since Kagi only deals with close prices, its chart is cleaner and less "noisy" than the candlestick chart. Importantly, there is a great variation in the information density. Candlesticks populate a lot of screen real estate to express movement, compared to Kagi lines. There is also a difference when locating Fibonacci resistance lines. There will be variations. Using Fibonacci resistance lines is very useful in trading, and therefore, when you are using Kagi charts with Fibonacci lines, also put Fibonacci lines on the candlestick version of the charts. When overlaying Fibonacci resistance lines on the candlesticks, the origin of any Fibonacci line will be a low or a high.

Figure 9.10 Four-Hour Kagi (L) and Candlestick (R) Charts, U.S. Treasury Bonds

Source: Chart copyright www.ProRealTime.com

CHAPTER 10

Point and Figure Charts

THE AIM OF this chapter is to present a review of the basic concepts and applications of point and figure charting to trading markets.

Point and figure charting represents the final chart type in our discussion of alternative charting. Like price break charts and Kagi charts, this chart type's origins precede the age of the computer. It is the only alternative chart type whose origin is in the West. In recent years, Thomas Dorsey has been a notable leader in applying point and figure charts to analysis of price movements. Jeremy Du Plessis, in the preface to *The Definitive Guide to Point and Figure* (Harriman House), states:

> [A]nyone wishing to practice technical analysis of the markets should be fully conversant with [point and figure charting]. [It] may be the oldest method of charting the market in the Western world, but that does not mean [it] should be ignored in our modern world. On the contrary, once you understand more about [it], you will wonder how you survived without [it].

How Point and Figure Charts Work

Point and figure charts work in the following way: When a price exceeds and closes at a predetermined distance up, it gets an X posted. If it reverses by three times the value of a prescribed number, it gets an O column. If a price exceeds a predetermined distance down, it gets an additional O posted, and if it reverses by three times the value of a prescribed number, it gets an X column. In point and figure charting this is known as a *1 x three-box reversal*. The common practice in point and figure charting is to use high/low as the setting instead of a close of the prices.

The following is the construction logic for point and figure charting. A flowchart of the logic appears as **Figure 10.1. Figure 10.2** depicts supplemental logic.

Point and Figure Chart Construction Logic

Point and Figure chart construction logic uses the series of definitions and formulae given below.

Low defines the current low price.

High defines the current high price.

ParentLow defines the previous low price.

ParentHigh defines the previous high price.

BoxCeiling(ParentHigh)

➤ Compute Quotient(ParentHigh, Box Size)

➤ **IF** (Quotient * Box Size) **EQUALS** ParentHigh **THEN** BoxCeiling(ParentHigh) = ParentHigh

ELSE BoxCeiling(ParentHigh) = (Quotient + 1) * Box Size

BoxCeiling(Low)

➤ Compute Quotient(Low, Box Size)

➤ **IF** (Quotient * Box Size) **EQUALS** Low **THEN** BoxCeiling (Low) = Low

ELSE BoxCeiling(Low) = (Quotient + 1) * Box Size

BoxFloor(ParentLow)

➤ Compute Quotient(ParentLow, BoxSize)

➤ BoxFloor(ParentLow) = Quotient * Box Size

BoxFloor(High)

➤ Compute Quotient(High, BoxSize)

➤ BoxFloor(High) = Quotient * Box Size

(Continued)

Point and Figure Chart Construction Logic (*Continued*)

Uptrend Flag

Set Uptrend Flag to TRUE if the expression

FLOOR((BoxFloor(High) – BoxCeiling(ParentHigh))/Box Size) **IS** GREATER THAN OR EQUAL TO 1

evaluates to TRUE.

Downtrend Flag

Set to TRUE if the expression

FLOOR((BoxFloor(ParentLow) – BoxCeiling(Low))/Box Size) **IS** GREATER THAN OR EQUAL TO 1

evaluates to TRUE.

Uptrend Plot Details

PLOT FROM BoxCeiling(ParentHigh) TO BoxFloor(High)

Symbol = 'X'

Symbol Count = (((BoxFloor(High) – BoxCeiling(ParentHigh))/ Box Size) + 1)

Trend Flag = Uptrend

Last Plot = BoxFloor(High)

Downtrend Plot Details

PLOT FROM BoxFloor(Parent Low) TO BoxCeiling(Low)

Symbol = 'O'

Symbol Count = (((BoxFloor(ParentLow) – BoxCeiling(Low))/ Box Size) + 1)

Trend Flag = Downtrend

Last Plot = BoxCeiling(Low)

Reversal Amount

Box Size * (# Box Reversals Required To Change Column)

Price Reversal

Uptrend Price Reversal = Last Plot – Reversal Amount

Downtrend Price Reversal = Last Plot + Reversal Amount

(*Continued*)

Point and Figure Chart Construction Logic (*Continued*)

User Input:

Accept user input or set default for the following:

➤ Read Box Size in basis points
➤ Read # Box Reversals Required To Change Column

Base Construction Logic:

1. Set Box Size, Reversal Amount
2. Set Column # to 1
3. Read Base Date, Base High Price, and Base Low Price
4. Read Next Date, Next High Price, and Next Low Price
5. Determine Uptrend or Downtrend and set the appropriate flag
6. IF Uptrend THEN follow **Uptrend Plot Details**
ELSE IF Downtrend THEN follow **Downtrend Plot Details**
ELSE *ignore price row* and set Trend Flag to null

Iterative Construction Logic:

1. Read Date, High Price, Low Price
2. Set Parent Row to Immediate Prior Non Ignored Row
3. **IF** previous and current trends are Uptrend **THEN**
Follow Uptrend Plot Details; and then go to step 1 of *Iterative Construction Logic.*
ELSE IF uptrend followed by Uptrend Price Reversal **THEN**
Follow Downtrend Plot Details; and then go to step 1 of *Iterative Construction Logic.*

ELSE

Set Trend Flag to <null>, ignore current row and go to step of *Iterative Construction Logic.*

4. **IF** previous and current trends are Downtrend **THEN**

Follow Downtrend Plot Details; and then go to step 1 of *Iterative Construction Logic.*
ELSE IF Downtrend followed by Downtrend Price Reversal **THEN**
Follow Uptrend Plot Details; and then go to step 1 of *Iterative Construction Logic.*

ELSE

Set Trend Flag to <null>, ignore current row and go to step 1 of *Iterative Construction Logic.*

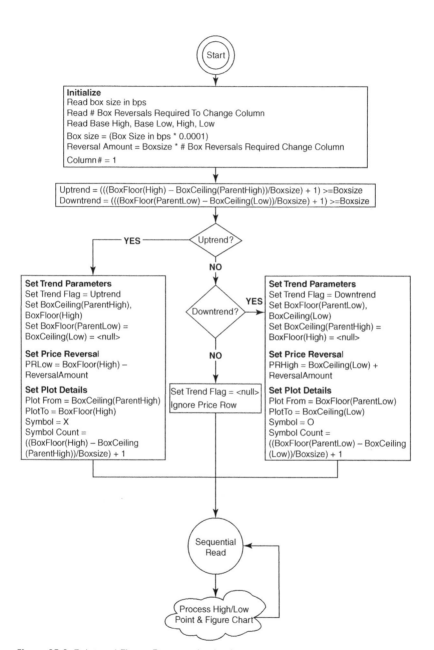

Figure 10.1 Point and Figure Construction Logic

Source: Abe Cofnas and Sridhar Iyer

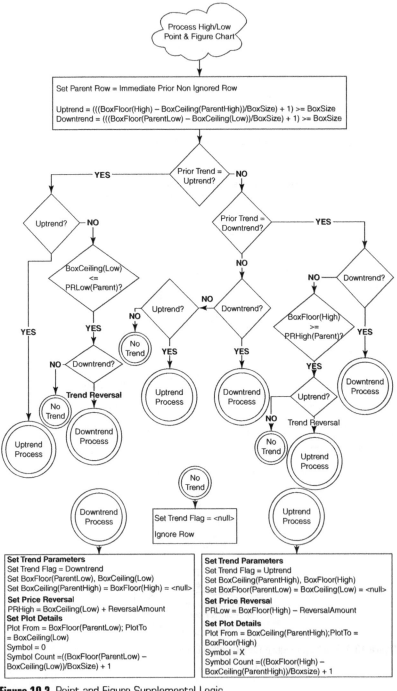

Figure 10.2 Point and Figure Supplemental Logic

Source: Abe Cofnas and Sridhar Iyer

Reversal Settings: When to Vary Them

Depending on what markets he is trading, the trader needs to make a choice of setting size. Determining the setting size is a very controversial subject because in many ways it is subjective. Basically, the setting size should be large enough to generate a pattern that is stable but small enough to reflect changes in sentiment. Too large will hide important moves, while too small will cause too many countertrends. It is a balancing act that we can quantify. At this stage in point and figure chart analysis, very few quantification and optimization studies have been done to determine the best increment for a setting. Most advisers stress that it is up to the personal judgment of the trader. However, what is really important is whether the reversals coincide with or confirm the projections derived from the other chart types. The central, unifying idea here is to have point and figure charts provide diversification in a trader's analysis. This means that the trader should compare point and figure charting to what other charts are displaying at the same time. Using point and figure charting in isolation is a suboptimal strategy, and is not enough to tap into its value. However, when we use it in combination with other charts, point and figure charting generates an enhanced identification of key support and resistance lines. We will shortly see how to integrate point and figure charts with the other chart signals. The settings are important because the setting amount greatly influences the ability of point and figure chart analysis to confirm other signals. If the trader is using a Kagi charts turnaround of 1 percent, the point and figure charts should be lower to allow for increased granularity in the outcome.

Setting Box Size as a Basis for Stop Strategies

The other significant value of the setting is its ability to generate stop strategies. For example, if a trader is trading and has an average profit of 1.50, the appearance of a reversal column could significantly dissipate that profit. A setting of .25 in these circumstances means that a price move of .75 would have to occur for an X column to become a Y column, or vice versa. If the trader selects the setting of .25, the risk of seeing half the profits disappear is greater. The question is when is this amount acceptable? Does the trader really want to accept a

50 percent loss of profits? If not, the setting needs to trigger a reversal. In this case, a setting of .10 would engender a reversal when a three-pip distance was traveled. This would leave much more of the profit protected. Such a strategy would mean that the trader could use point and figure charts as an alert to lighten up or get out of a position when a reversal occurred. Can we use a reversal column as an entry indicator? The answer is that it depends on where the reversal occurred. If it occurs at a confluence of a key Fibonacci resistance line, it makes sense to use it as such. If it occurs in the middle of a range, joining a reversal column doesn't make sense.

We will also show that point and figure chart reversal columns, when considered together with price break charts and Kagi charts, can enhance the confidence of a trader to enter the position.

Variations in Settings in Selected Markets

Point and figure charts have great visual attractiveness. The Xs and the Os provide a clarity not present with candlesticks. Even more important is the gain in clarity about market sentiment when the box sizes vary. Let's review some sample markets and see what happens with box size changes.

Gold Day Chart Compared to Ten-Minute Chart

Point and figure chart settings should also vary based on the time intervals selected. For example, it makes sense to use a wider setting to capture significant moves, whereas in an intraday ten-minute chart one would reduce the point and figure chart box size to allow for detection of smaller waves of sentiment. The 1 percent box size **(Figure 10.3)** works well for the gold day chart, but a 0.05 or one-half of 1 percent size **(Figure 10.4)** allows the trader to see more detail in gold movements.

Crude Oil and Point and Figure Charts

Crude oil traders applying point and figure charts would set the box size interval to the amount they expect to profit on the average. Let's assume a ninety-cent move satisfies a trader. In that case, if a reversal column

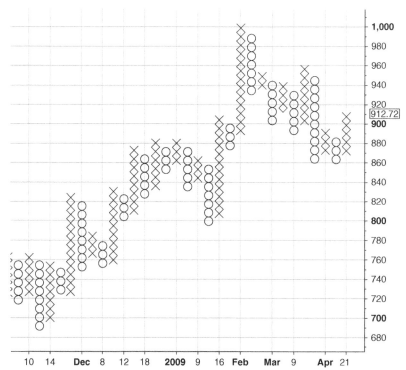

Figure 10.3 Gold Spot Point and Figure Box, Size = 1%, Time Interval = Day
Source: Chart copyright www.ProRealTime.com

appeared, a box size of ten cents (0.10) would generate a pullback of 30 cents. This threat to the profits could cause some traders to lighten up before the profit turned to a loss. Additionally, a ten-cent box size would enable more precise detection of oil movements at even a fifteen-minute basis **(Figure 10.5)**.

As **Figure 10.6** shows, point and figure charts make it relatively easy to find common patterns such as trend lines, channels, tops, and bottoms. As in other charting types, these classical tools used with a point and figure chart enhance identification of key boundaries where signals are generated. Point and figure charts act as maps of sentiment by quickly providing not only support and resistance line levels but also the contours of the battle between buyers and sellers. Traders can therefore use point and figure charting as a Geiger counter of sentiment, because it detects an increase in the seismic levels of the friction and combat between bulls and bears.

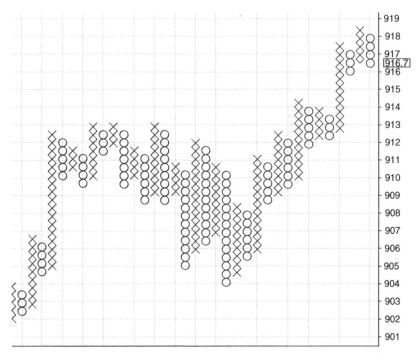

Figure 10.4 Gold Spot Point and Figure Box, Size = 0.05%, Time Interval =
Ten Minutes
Source: Chart copyright www.ProRealTime.com

The Horizontal Count

One technique for getting an estimate of the potential move after a break
out in point and figure charts is the *horizontal count*. Tom Dorsey, one
of the leaders in point and figure analysis, sets forth the rule as follows:

> Simply count the number of boxes horizontally at the widest point
> of formation. That number is multiplied by 3 and the product
> of that multiplication is again multiplied by the box size. Then
> add the product of this multiplication to the lowest point of
> formation.[1]

Dorsey also sets forth a risk rule: "You should have at least two
points of potential profit for each point potential loss before initiating
a trade."[2] (Dorsey, T. [2001]. *Point and Figure Charting*. Indianapolis:
John Wiley & Sons.)

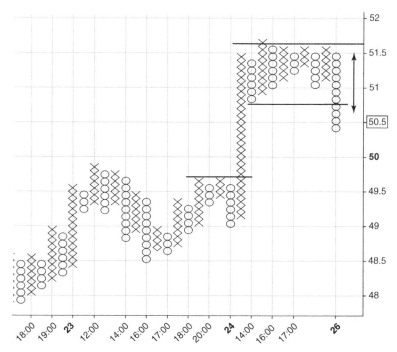

Figure 10.5 Crude Oil Point and Figure Box (June 2009), Size = Ten cents,
Time Interval = Fifteen Minutes

Source: Chart copyright www.ProRealTime.com

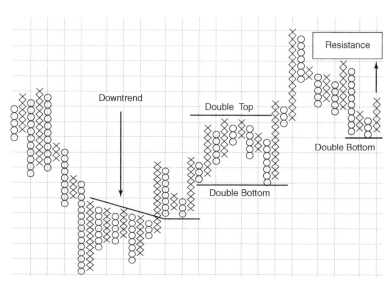

Figure 10.6 Common Patterns in Point and Figure

Source: Chart copyright www.ProRealTime.com

Fibonacci Resistance Levels and Point and Figure Charts

Fibonacci resistance levels work well with point and figure charts. The trader will find that long columns of Xs or Os often reverse halfway and then reverse again. This is characteristic of Fibonacci resistance lines-based behavior. The addition of Fibonacci resistance lines provides an enhanced signal on entry (**Figure 10.7**). If an X breaks out above a Fibonacci resistance line, or if an O breaks below a Fibonacci resistance line, it is a more reliable break than it would be at other locations.

The Dollar Index and Point and Figure Charts

The dollar index plays an important role in trading currency and commodity markets. It is used as a gauge of dollar sentiment. A trader or investor who scans the dollar index is looking for answers to several

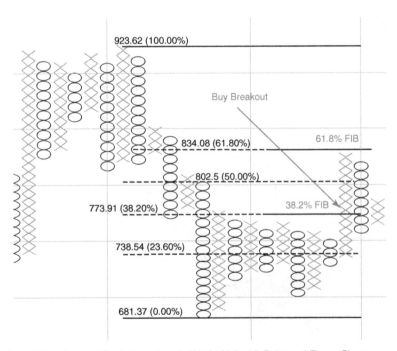

Figure 10.7 Fibonacci Resistance Levels Work Well with Point and Figure Charts
Source: Chart copyright www.ProRealTime.com

key questions. First, what is the prevailing direction being visualized? Second, what is the strength of that direction? Finally, are there signals for entry or exit? "What is the prevailing direction?" is not such an easy question to answer. The answer depends upon where one starts. The starting location depends upon one's strategic viewpoint. If the trader is looking for a long-term strategy, looking at the whole set of columns is the best way to view it **(Figure 10.8)**. In contrast, a short-term trader would focus on the most recent column **(Figure 10.9)**. The best approach is to find the most recent significant low or high and evaluate the patterns from that point of view. In our example, the prevailing direction is down, and we see that the DXY broke down with a new low O. But it is useful to keep in mind that the trader should zoom into a smaller time frame. By doing so, one can see in the DXY that the breakdown was encountering a bounce up when the trader viewed the intraday time frame.

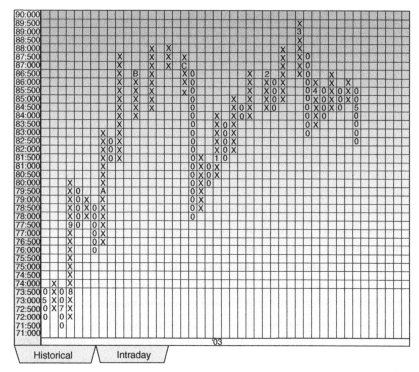

Figure 10.8 Dollar Index, May 11 to May 12, 2009, Historical View
Source: Bloomberg

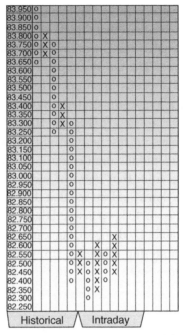

Figure 10.9 Dollar Index, May 11 to May 12, 2009, Intraday View
Source: Bloomberg

Strength of Direction

What is the strength of the direction, and how do point and figure charts show it? Asking this question provides valuable insights into the nature of the sentiment being expressed. With point and figure charts, one can quickly perceive variations in trend strength, strength of a countertrend move, and significant support or resistance. This makes point and figure charting the tool for those who are occupying the middle ground of trading, neither too big nor too small a time frame. Trend strength and its variations are quickly indicated by the length of the column, as well as the frequency of reversals. Of course, one may expect a long column to be followed by a shorter countermove. Here is where point and figure charts provide an edge. As long as the alternating columns do not take out outer resistance and support lines that are in effect, they simply signal a consolidation in the prices. The battle between the bulls and the bears, in such cases, has entered a neutral zone. No one is winning until there is a break out. It is at the break points that optimal trading occurs. Therefore, breakouts are important areas of focus for the trader.

Let's consider several examples. In the point and figure chart in **Figure 10.10** we see an overall down trend. There is a large drop in the O column but it is followed by a retracement and a sequence of alternating Xs and Os. The trend is up from the vantage point of looking from the double bottoms of the two-O column to the latest. Yet the path through it is far from consistent. The trader looking at the most recent column, although he sees that an X column in effect, would not conclude that there is an uptrend, but rather would simply detect a prevailing bullish mood.

Point and figure chart patterns coincide easily with the use of classical trend lines. Once a trend line is placed along a plane of Xs or Os, in effect the trader is identifying buying and selling zones. In addition, there is a momentum aspect of the trend line that is important in point and figure: the angle of the trend line. The chart in Figure 10.10 shows

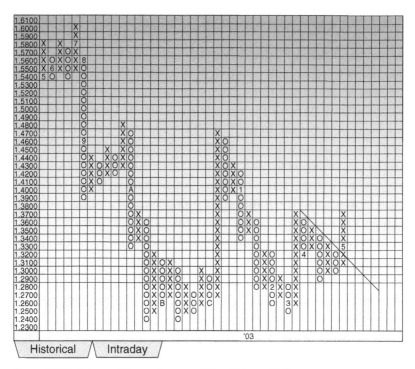

Figure 10.10 Point and Figure Charts and Trend Lines: 45 Degrees

Source: Bloomberg

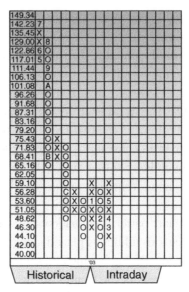

Figure 10.11 Double Bottoms Signify Strong Support

Source: Bloomberg

an important pattern—the downtrend line being broken. Also, notice that the O box that broke down went through a 45-degree angle. This provides an additional dimension of momentum: two X boxes up for every one down. When a 45-degree line is penetrated, it is an extra signal of a break in the trend. In the EURUSD point and figure chart (Figure 10.10) we see a case where the trend line is in fact a 45-degree line tracking the progression of lower X columns. When one can draw such a line, it represents a strong sentiment wave. In this example, a bearish barrier, when broken, should be considered a strong signal of a bullish retreat. In **Figure 10.11** we can see a most interesting quadruple bottom!

In **Figure 10.12**, we see an example of double-top X columns appearing in a crude oil chart. These provide an unambiguous signature of strong resistance. Conversely, double bottoms, when formed by aligned O columns that have stopped going down, would show strong support.

Combining Chart Types

We have now come to the core concept of this book. Most users of point and figure charts, price break charts, Kagi charts, or Renko

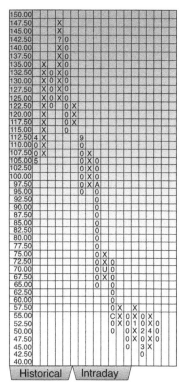

Figure 10.12 Double-Top X Columns Signify Strong Resistance

Source: Bloomberg

charts apply these charts in a very narrow and myopic way. They select the one they are most familiar with and ignore the others. While each charting technique has, as we have seen, its own features, none can be a total substitute for any other. Therefore, what would make better sense would be to depart from this approach, instead using these alternative charting methods together and integrating the results of their calculations. The impact of such integration is that it adds extra levels of granularity to the view of the price action. There are two ways to accomplish this goal of comparative evaluation of chart types and their integration. The first approach is to conduct a surface visual analysis. The trader, in addition to viewing the common candlestick pattern, would have two or more different screens with price break charts, Kagi charts, Renko charts, and point and figure charts. Each screen would become, in effect, an analytical surface. A visual scan of all the charts at the same time would enable the trader to eyeball new signals and areas of interest quickly. In effect, such a comparative scan would generate new price landmarks. To date, few traders have done this because such scanning required multiple screens. Because screen technology has become cost-effective, few serious traders now trade with less than two screens, and as a result, the strategy of comparative scanning is now easy to accomplish.

The second approach, which we demonstrate shortly, is to integrate and compare these charts not as charts, but within a price data matrix. We call the resulting table of values the Price Landmark Matrix. Such a matrix lets the trader identify important correlated areas of interest in each chart type, *without needing a chart*. There is another significant benefit of an integrated approach. It allows a trader to analyze bullish and bearish conditions quickly. Those who have a bullish orientation to a trade can seek multiple confirmations of whether the sentiment is bullish across all the alternative charts. Those who have a bearish orientation to a trade can confirm, by viewing multiple charts, whether that scenario is playing out as well among the price break, point and figure, Renko, Kagi, and candlestick charts.

Let's first discuss the visual analysis path of comparing all the types at the same time. Thereafter we will review the structure and use of the Price Landmark Matrix.

The first step in applying a visual comparison is to find the key support and resistance lines generated by each chart tool and tag them on the chart itself. Here are several examples.

S&P 500 Cash Day Chart

In the multichart view of the S&P 500 (**Figure 10.13**), you can see the various resistance and support lines on the point and figure chart, Kagi chart, and price break chart on the top panel. The trader can review the key landmarks. The important question to ask is whether the differing "landmarks" confirm or contradict the intended trade. One can align both a bullish and a bearish scenario with the shape of these alternative charts. A bullish scenario would point to the presence of an X column on the point and figure chart. The point and figure chart shows a sequence of higher X columns. The Kagi chart shows a sequence of higher waists and a recent turn from a Yin to a Yang. The price break charts shows that

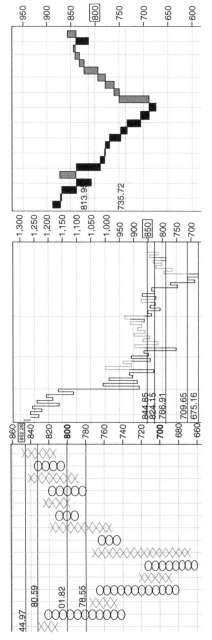

Figure 10.13 S&P Cash Multichart View: Point and Figure Chart, Kagi Chart, and Price Break Chart

Source: Bloomberg

173

the S&P had experienced a sequence of eight consecutive high closes followed by one reversal, which flip-flopped back. This is a strong confirmation that a bullish sentiment remains strong. On the other hand, one can formulate a bearish strategy not as one that calls for immediately joining the action, but as one that waits for bearish conditions to emerge on these charts. Using the point and figure chart, we see inner support at 801.82 and outer support at 779.55. The Kagi charts show support at 786.91 and outer support at 675.15. The price break charts show inner support at 813.95 and outer support near 675.

Notice that there is variation in the confirmed support levels from these different charts. Each chart gives the trader different landmarks for sellers looking for a breakdown trade. For example, the point and figure conditions for a sell entry would be the emergence of an O column on point and figure charts. The Kagi chart conditions for a sell entry would be the turning of Yang to Yin. The price break chart conditions for a sell entry would be a reversal down on the price break charts. Each strategy has alternative price action scripts that might occur. It is always in the trader's best interest to anticipate the different possible scenarios that the price path may take. This seems obvious, but few traders do it.

Multiple Views of Gold

The display of spot gold (**Figures 10.14** through **10.16**) in the various chart styles also reveals how these charts differ in their display of the density of information. The Kagi chart shows with ease an entire year of trading, using a setting of one month, compared to the candlestick chart, which shows one and one-half months in the same amount of chart real estate. The point and figure chart columns further condense prices to provide an easy-to-obtain big-picture view of sentiment. The price break charts give approximately the same density of information per time period as the point and figure charts.

The price landmarks generated by each chart vary. The Kagi chart shows support at 867.97 and a recent breakdown of support at 894.50. The candlesticks are very choppy, with difficult-to-measure support and resistance.

These four charts are inconclusive about who is in control. The sentiment is bullish, and an X column has just been initiated. However, the price break chart confirms that gold at the hard right edge had a reversal break down and is in a bearish sequence.

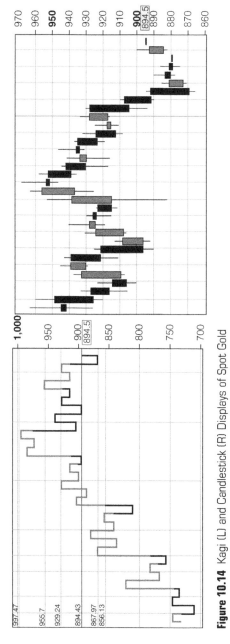

Figure 10.14 Kagi (L) and Candlestick (R) Displays of Spot Gold

Source: Chart copyright www.ProRealTime.com

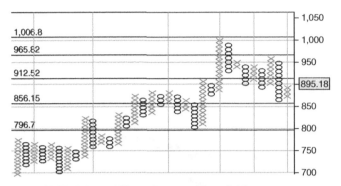

Figure 10.15 Point and Figure Display of Spot Gold
Source: Chart copyright www.ProRealTime.com

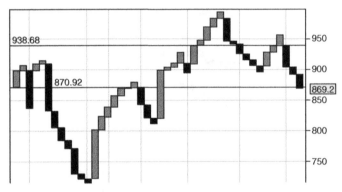

Figure 10.16 Price Break Display of Spot Gold
Source: Chart copyright www.ProRealTime.com

Multiple Views of Oil

A four-panel view of crude oil **(Figure 10.17)** shows how chart variations generate different points of support, resistance lines, and projected buy and sell zones. Here we see crude oil forming a triangle with the candlestick charts, with the price of 50 as support. The Kagi chart confirms a similar triangle and shows a Kagi waistline for support at 50. The point and figure chart shows an outer support line at 49.

Multiple Views of S&P Cash One-Minute Charts

In **Figures 10.18** through **10.20**, we see S&P cash price break, point and figure candlestick, and Kagi charts using a one-minute

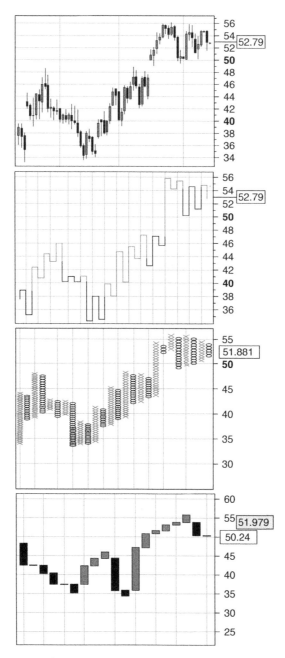

Figure 10.17 Four-Panel View of Crude Oil

Source: Chart copyright www.ProRealTime.com

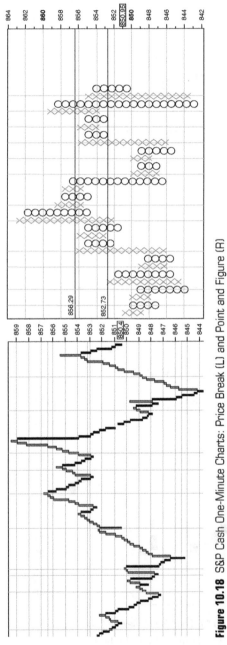

Figure 10.18 S&P Cash One-Minute Charts: Price Break (L) and Point and Figure (R)

Source: Chart copyright www.ProRealTime.com

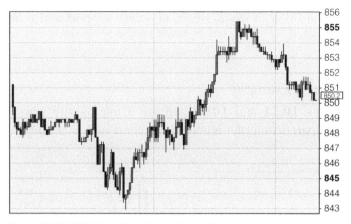

Figure 10.19 S&P Cash One-Minute Chart: Candlestick
Source: Chart copyright www.ProRealTime.com

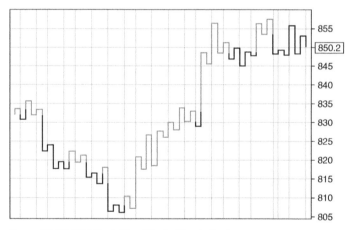

Figure 10.20 S&P Cash One-Minute Chart: Kagi
Source: Chart copyright www.ProRealTime.com

pattern. Let's start with the price break chart. The price break chart shows a reversal down at the hard right edge. Therefore, we can immediately see that a downtrend is in place. More importantly, the price break chart reversal point was projected to be at 953.18. The point and figure chart had a projected breakdown at 852.73. At the same time, the Kagi chart shows 845.00 as the landmark for support. Once again, we see how all three provided an additional view, beyond that of candlesticks, of where support and resistance lines occurred.

One-Minute Example

In **Figures 10.21** and **10.22**, we see a one-minute price break chart compared to a one-minute Kagi chart with a setting of 0.10.

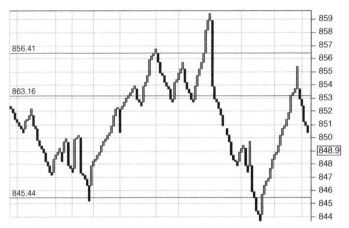

Figure 10.21 One-Minute Price Break Chart
Source: Chart copyright www.ProRealTime.com

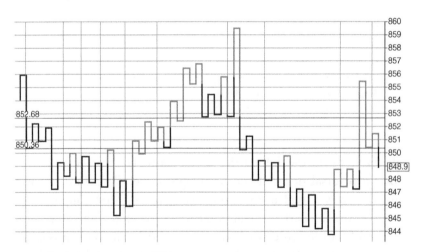

Figure 10.22 One-Minute Kagi Chart
Source: Chart copyright www.ProRealTime.com

We have seen that price break charts can project a breakout reversal. A breakout reversal at 856.41 was projected for April 14 at 13.12. The Kagi chart showed support at 852.56, which was projectable on April 14 at 12:26. The breakdown occurred below this, on April 14 at 13.28. In this case, the Kagi chart signal was the earlier by twenty minutes. Differences such as these can add up to a great deal of money.

Chapter Notes

1. Thomas Dorsey, *Point and Figure Charting*, Second Edition. Indianapolis: Wiley, 2007.
2. Ibid.

CHAPTER 11

Integrating Price
Break, Kagi,
Renko, and Point
and Figure Charting

THE AIM OF this chapter is to present a framework for integrating price break, Kagi, Renko, and point and figure charting without needing to view each chart. The result is a useful trading analysis and alert tool. The reader will learn how to combine the power of all these charting methods to identify key price landmarks, multiple entry points, and confirming signals. We will also introduce the concept of the Price Landmark Matrix analytical tool.

Using the Price Landmark Matrix

The best way to unleash the power of simultaneous use of price break charts, Kagi charts, point and figure charts, and Renko charts is to create a Price Landmark Matrix. This innovation, which combines data integration and design, identifies the key signals coming from these four charts. Since many traders do not have access to all or some of these charts, the Price Landmark Matrix concept provides an alternative. It scans the open, high, low, and close price data in the candlestick charts and converts the data, using appropriate construction logic, into multiple alerts in a data table format. This concept allows the trader to have the advantage of using alternative charts without actually having to display them.

Let's explore how this works with data for different instruments. We will demonstrate the Price Landmark Matrix for the EURUSD, gold, crude oil, DAX, and S&P. In principle, we can use it for any instrument.

First, we will review the key structure of the Price Landscape Matrix. (Note: All data in these examples comes from Bloomberg L.P.)

Components of the Price Landmark Matrix

Section 1: Raw Price Data

The Price Landmark Matrix is a database spreadsheet constructed so that the trader can access different views of the data associated with price break, Kagi, Renko, and point and figure charts. There are several components of this matrix. The first section details user inputs. User inputs will vary for each type of chart. This is the area for input of those user settings. For price break charts it is the number of lines that are counted as a reversal point; for Renko charts it is brick size; for Kagi charts it is the turnaround amount; and for point and figure charts it is the box size and reversal setting.

A second matrix component is the raw price data. This section is where the price data is stored and displayed.

The third component is a process section that displays an inventory of key information used as input for programming the charts: date, open, high, low, and close **(Figure 11.1)**. This area is of importance to traders who want to program their own charts.

[EURUSD RPD] RAW PRICE DATA

Date	Open	High	Low	Close
10/23/2007	1.4181	1.4279	1.4172	1.4263
10/22/2007	1.4280	1.4348	1.4126	1.4181
10/19/2007	1.4294	1.4319	1.4245	1.4301
10/18/2007	1.4207	1.4310	1.4197	1.4295
10/17/2007	1.4172	1.4230	1.4158	1.4208
10/16/2007	1.4204	1.4226	1.4144	1.4173
10/15/2007	1.4130	1.4243	1.4130	1.4205
10/12/2007	1.4196	1.4213	1.4154	1.4178
10/11/2007	1.4145	1.4241	1.4136	1.4196
10/10/2007	1.4105	1.4171	1.4094	1.4145
10/9/2007	1.4047	1.4113	1.4015	1.4106
10/8/2007	1.4138	1.4154	1.4036	1.4048

Base Data

Figure 11.1 Raw Data—Price Landmark Matrix
Source: Bloomberg

Thereafter the Price Landmark Matrix has sections devoted to each alternative chart and key landmarks related to each chart.

Section 2: Price Break Chart Components

This section displays several columns relating to price break charts. The process section for price break charts (**Figure 11.2**) includes:

➤ **Price Movement:** Indicates whether price is going up or down.
➤ **Price Reversal:** Indicates if a reversal has occurred.
➤ **Box Low Close:** Indicates where the low close occurred.
➤ **Box High Close:** Indicates where the high close occurred.
➤ **Price Break Box ID:** Indicates to which number in the sequence the box corresponds.

[PB IS] INPUT SECTION		[PB PS] PROCESS SECTION (For Programmers)				
[PB EURUSD] Raw Data		[PB FM] Price Movement	[PB 3PBR] 3 Price Break Reversal?	[PB BLC] Box Low Close	[PB BHC] Box High Close	[PB BID] Price Break Box ID
[PB D] Date	[PB C] Close					
10/23/2007	1.4263	Up	No	1.4181	1.4263	
10/22/2007	1.4181	Down	Yes	1.4181	1.4295	Box8
10/19/2007	1.4301	Up		1.4295	1.4301	Box7
10/18/2007	1.4295	Up		1.4208	1.4295	Box6
10/17/2007	1.4208	Up		1.4205	1.4208	Box5
10/16/2007	1.4173	Down	No	1.4173	1.4205	
10/15/2007	1.4205	Up		1.4196	1.4205	Box4
10/12/2007	1.4178	Down	No	1.4178	1.4196	
10/11/2007	1.4196	Up		1.4145	1.4196	Box3
10/10/2007	1.4145	Up		1.4106	1.4145	Box2
10/9/2007	1.4106	Up		1.4048	1.4106	Box1

Figure 11.2 Process Section: Price Break Chart
Source: Abe Cofnas and Sridhar Iyer

The Price Landmark Map section (**Figure 11.3**) includes but is not limited to:

➤ Completed Number of Consecutive Highs/Lows (tells how far into a sequence the reversal column is).
➤ Next Reversal Price.
➤ Recommended Entry Strategy (identifies locations for a buy or sell).
➤ Distance Beyond Breakpoint to Low Close.
➤ Distance Beyond Breakpoint to High Close.
➤ Average of the Distance Beyond Breakpoint to Low Close.
➤ Average of the Distance Beyond Breakpoint to High Close.
➤ Number of Up Reversals from Start Date.
➤ Number of Down Reversals from Start Date.
➤ Average Sequence of Consecutive High Closes in Up Reversal.
➤ Average Sequence of Consecutive Down Closes in Down Reversal.

Section Three: Kagi Chart Components

The Kagi charts section of the Price Landmark Matrix (**Figure 11.4a and Figure 11.4b**) displays key elements of the data from the vantage point of Kagi chart analysis. Kagi chart raw price data uses closes only, so you don't see the other data on open, high, and low. Also included are user-setting inputs where the user sets the fixed reversal amount and the distance above or below the Kagi shoulder needed to trigger an order. These include:

➤ Date
➤ Close (closing price)
➤ Line Tip Price (the price where the Yang or Yin price would begin)
➤ Reversal Amount at Line Tip (the minimum needed to generate a Yin or Yang)

The next columns in the Price Landmark Map section deal with key descriptions of the price data:

➤ Yin
➤ Yang

[PB IS] INPUT SECTION   [PB PLM] PRICE LANDMARK MAP SECTION

[PB D] Date	[PB C] Close	[PB CHL] Completed Number of Consecutive Highs/Lows	[PB NRP] Next Reversal Price	[PB H] # of Consecutive Highs	[PB L] # of Consecutive Lows	[PB RES] Recommended Entry Strategy	[PB BLC] Distance Beyond Breakpoint To Low Close	[PB BHC] Distance Beyond Breakpoint To High Close	[PB ABLC] Average of the Distance Beyond Breakpoint To Low Close	[PB ABHC] Average of the Distance Beyond Breakpoint To High Close	[PB UR] # Up Reversals From Start Date	[PB DR] # Down Reversals From Start Date	[PB HCUR] Average Sequence of Consecutive High Closes in Up Reversal	[PB DCDR] Average Sequence of Consecutive Down Closes in Down Reversal
10/23/2007	1.4263													
10/22/2007	1.4181	1L			1		0.0024		0.0024		1		7	
10/19/2007	1.4301	7H	1.4205	7		Sell on break below 1.4205								
10/18/2007	1.4295	6H	1.4196	6		Sell on break below 1.4196								
10/17/2007	1.4208	5H	1.4145	5		Sell on break below 1.4145								

(Continued)

187

[PB IS] INPUT SECTION | [PB PLM] PRICE LANDMARK MAP SECTION

[PB D] Date	[PB C] Close	[PB CHL] Completed Number of Consecutive Highs/Lows	[PB NRP] Next Reversal Price	[PB H] # of Consecutive Highs	[PB L] # of Consecutive Lows	[PB RES] Recommended Entry Strategy	[PB BLC] Distance Beyond Breakpoint To Low Close	[PB BHC] Distance Beyond Breakpoint To High Close	[PB ABLC] Average of the Distance Beyond Breakpoint To Low Close	[PB ABHC] Average of the Distance Beyond Breakpoint To High Close	[PB UR] # Up Reversals From Start Date	[PB DR] # Down Reversals From Start Date	[PB HCUR] Average Sequence of Consecutive High Closes in Up Reversal	[PB DCDR] Average Sequence of Consecutive Down Closes in Down Reversal
10/16/2007	1.4173													
10/15/2007	1.4205	4H	1.4106	4		Sell on break below 1.4106								
10/12/2007	1.4178													
10/11/2007	1.4196	3H	1.4048	3		Sell on break below 1.4048								
10/10/2007	1.4145	2H		2										
10/9/2007	1.4106	1H		1										

Figure 11.3 Price Landmark Map Section: Price Break Chart

Source: Bloomberg

188

➤ Number of Consecutive
- Shoulder/High
- Waist/Low
➤ Shoulder Price Turning Point
➤ Projected Buy Signal (Yin to Yang)
➤ Waist Price Turning Point
➤ Projected Sell Signal (Yang to Yin)
➤ Ratio of Yin Length over Yang Length

Section 4: Renko Chart Components

The Renko chart Price Landmark Matrix (**Figures 11.4a and 11.4b**) is composed of input, process, and price landmark sections that display relevant Renko chart information. This includes, but is not limited to

➤ User settings for brick size
➤ Date
➤ Close price
➤ Number of bricks in sequence
➤ Brick color
➤ Next black brick
➤ Next gray brick
➤ Number of bricks drawn
➤ Brick color
➤ Next support breakpoint
➤ Next resistance breakpoint
➤ Bricks per minute

Point and Figure Chart Components

For point and figure charts, the same price data is organized and displayed in specialized columns (**Figures 11.5–11.7**) that include, but are not limited to:

➤ Box Size (user setting for box size)
➤ # Box Reversals (price reversal setting)
➤ Date
➤ High
➤ Low

[K IS] INPUT SECTION		[K PS] PROCESS SECTION (For Programmers)					[K PLM] PRICE LANDMARK MAP SECTION								
[K PRA] Fixed Percentage Reversal Amount		0.1													
[K DAS] Distance above Shoulder(High) in bps		5													
[K DBW] Distance below Waist(Low) in bps		5													
[K EURUSD] Raw Data				Turn-around Price Decision Price at Line Tip **[K TPL]**		Classification **[K CL]**		Number of Consecutive **[K NC]**							
[K D] Date	**[K C]** Close	**[K LTP]** Line Tip Price	**[K RALT]** Reversal Amount At Line Tip	**[K L]** Low	**[K H]** High	**[K YIN]** Yin	**[K YANG]** Yang	**[K S]** Shoulder/High	**[K W]** Waist/Low	**[K SPTP]** Shoulder Price Turning Point	**[K PBS]** Projected Buy Signal (Yin to Yang)	**[K WPTP]** Waist Price Turning Point	**[K PSS]** Projected Sell Signal (Yang to Yin)	**[K RYY]** Ratio of Yin Length over Yang Length
10/23/2007	1.4263	1.4263	0.0014263	1.4248737	1.4277		Up		3			1.4181		
10/22/2007	1.4181	1.4181	0.0014181	1.4166819	1.4195		Down	3		1.4301	1.4205			33.33%
10/19/2007	1.4301	1.4301	0.0014301	1.4286699	1.4315		Up							
10/18/2007	1.4295	1.4295	0.0014295	1.4280705	1.4309		Up							
10/17/2007	1.4208	1.4208	0.0014208	1.4193792	1.4222		Up		2			1.4173		18.52%
10/16/2007	1.4173	1.4173	0.0014173	1.4158827	1.4187	Down		2		1.4205			1.4178	

190

10/15/2007	1.4205	1.4205	0.0014205	1.4190795	1.4219	Up	1		1.4178
10/12/2007	1.4178	1.4178	0.0014178	1.4163822	1.4192	Down	1	1.4196	
10/11/2007	1.4196	1.4196	0.0014196	1.4181804	1.4210	Up			
10/10/2007	1.4145	1.4145	0.0014145	1.4130855	1.4159	Up			
10/9/2007	1.4106	1.4106	0.0014106	1.4091894	1.4120	Up			
10/8/2007	1.4048	1.4048	0.0014048	1.4033952	1.4062				

Base Close

Figure 11.4a Price Landmark Section: Renko Chart

Source: Bloomberg

[R IS] INPUT SECTION			[R PS] PROCESS SECTION (For Programmers)					[R PLM] PRICE LANDMARK MAP SECTION					
[R BS] Brick Setting in bps	10			[R IC] Intraday Calculations						[R DCD] Display Chart Details	[R BM] # Bricks per Time Unit (Brick Momentum)	[R BC] Brick Color	[R NSB] Next Support Breakpoint	[R NRB] Next Resistance Breakpoint
[R EURUSD] Raw Data														
[R D] Date	[R C] Close	[R BIS] # Bricks in Sequence	[R BC] Brick Color	[R NBB] Next Black Brick	[R NGB] Next Grey Brick									
10/23/2007	1.4263	6	Grey	1.4248	1.4258	10/23/2007	6	Grey	11 Black	
10/22/2007	1.4181	10	Black	1.4188	1.4198	10/22/2007	10	Black		12 Grey
10/19/2007	1.4301	1	Grey	1.4288	1.4298	10/19/2007	11	Grey	2 Black	
10/18/2007	1.4295	8	Grey	1.4278	1.4288					
10/17/2007	1.4208	2	Grey	1.4198	1.4208					
10/16/2007	1.4173	1	Black	1.4178	1.4188	10/16/2007	1	Black		2 Grey
10/15/2007	1.4205	1	Grey	1.4188	1.4198	10/15/2007	1	Grey		15 Grey
10/12/2007	1.4178	0		1.4178	1.4188	10/12/2007	0			
10/11/2007	1.4196	5	Grey	1.4178	1.4188	10/11/2007	14	Grey		
10/10/2007	1.4145	4	Grey	1.4128	1.4138					
10/9/2007	1.4106	5	Grey	1.4088	1.4098					
10/8/2007	1.4048	0		1.4048	1.4048	10/8/2007				

Base Close

Figure 11.4b Price Landmark Section: Renko Chart

Source: Bloomberg

➤ Chart Price
➤ Symbol Plot Columns
➤ Breakout X
➤ Breakdown O
➤ Highest X
➤ Lowest O
➤ Trend Flag (trend direction)
➤ Next Uptrend Value OR Box Ceiling
➤ Next Uptrend Value OR Box Low

[PAF IS] INPUT SECTION	
[PAF BS] Box Size (in bps)	10
[PAF BRR] # Box Reversals Required To Change Column	3

[PAF EURUSD] Raw Data		
[PAF D] Date	[PAF H] High	[PAF L] Low
10/23/2007	1.4279	1.4172
10/22/2007	1.4348	1.4126
10/19/2007	1.4319	1.4245
10/18/2007	1.4310	1.4197
10/17/2007	1.4230	1.4158
10/16/2007	1.4226	1.4144
10/15/2007	1.4243	1.4130
10/12/2007	1.4213	1.4154
10/11/2007	1.4241	1.4136
10/10/2007	1.4171	1.4094
10/9/2007	1.4113	1.4015
10/8/2007	1.4154	1.4036
Base		

Figure 11.5 Input Section: Point and Figure Chart
Source: Bloomberg

		[PAF PLM] PRICE LANDMARK MAP SECTION				
[PAF CP] Chart Price	[PAF SPC] Symbol Plot Columns		[PAF BX] Break- out X	[PAF BO] Break- down O	[PAF HX] Highest X	[PAF LO] Lowest O
	1 2 3 4 5 6					
1.4310	X				1.4310	
1.4300	X O					
1.4290	X O					
1.4280	X O					
1.4270	X O X					
1.4260	X O X					
1.4250	X O X		1.4250			
1.4240	X X O X					
1.4230	X O X O X					
1.4220	X O X O X					
1.4210	X O X O X					
1.4200	X O X O X					
1.4190	X O X O X					
1.4180	X O X O X					
1.4170	X O X O X					
1.4160	X O X O X					
1.4150	X O X O X					
1.4140	X O X O X					
1.4130	X O O X					
1.4120	X O			1.4120		1.4120
1.4110	X					
1.4100	X					
1.4090	X					
1.4080	X					
1.4070	X					
1.4060	X					
1.4050	X					
1.4040	X					
1.4030	O X					
1.4020	O					

Figure 11.6 Price Landmark Map Section: Point and Figure Chart
Source: Bloomberg

[PAF PS] PROCESS SECTION (For Programmers)

[PAF TF] Trend Flag	[PAF UP] Uptrend Parameters		[PAF DP] Downtrend Parameters		[PAF LP] Last Plot	[PAF PR] Price Reversal		[PAF SC] Symbol Count	[PAF PS] Plot Symbol	[PAF CN] Column Number
	[PAF NUV] Next Uptrend Value OR BoxCeiling (ParentHigh)	[PAF BFH] BoxFloor(High)	[PAF NDV] Next Downtrend Value OR BoxFloor (ParentLow)	[PAF BCL] BoxCeiling(Low)		[PAF H] High	[PAF L] Low			
Uptrend	1.4130	1.4270			1.4270		1.4240	15	X	6
Downtrend			1.4240	1.4120	1.4120	1.4150		13	O	5
Downtrend			1.4300	1.4250	1.4250	1.4280		6	O	5
Uptrend	1.4240	1.4310			1.4310		1.4280	8	X	4
Uptrend	1.4230	1.4230			1.4230		1.4200	1	X	4
Uptrend	1.4140	1.4220			1.4220		1.4190	9	X	4
Downtrend			1.4150	1.4130	1.4130	1.4160		3	O	3
Downtrend			1.4230	1.4160	1.4160	1.4190		8	O	3
Uptrend	1.4180	1.4240			1.4240		1.4210	7	X	2
Uptrend	1.4030	1.4170			1.4170		1.4140	15	X	2
Downtrend			1.4030	1.4020	1.4020	1.4050		2	O	1

Figure 11.7 Process Section: Point and Figure Chart

Source: Bloomberg

➤ Next Downtrend Value OR Box Floor
➤ Box Ceiling Low
➤ Last Plot
➤ Price Reversal: High
➤ Price Reversal: Low
➤ Symbol Count
➤ Plot Symbol

The Price Landmark Matrix Map:
A Visual Path Analysis

The central idea underlying the Price Landmark Matrix is that each chart type provides one or more key alerts. These alerts will be projections about trend direction, location of support and resistance lines, shifts in sentiment, and so on. The differences among the alerts generated arise because each chart's method of construction follows a different logic. Each chart captures the price data in Price Break Charts, Kagi Charts, Point and Figure Charts, or Renko Charts shapes. The Price Landmark Matrix Map is able to display any and all of the four charts. The result is a fresh view of the price action from the different perspectives of these charts.

The Price Landmark Matrix Map (**Figure 11.8**) is composed of several displays. On the left side is a display of a raw price data chart, price break chart, and Kagi chart. In the center is a display of the raw price data. At the center top is the Renko chart of the raw price data, and on the right side is the point and figure chart conversion of the raw price data. These displays can be on one screen or on multiple screens. Most importantly, this tool provides the trader with the equivalent of an X-ray or MRI of the price action. This kind of deep analysis has not been done before.

By converting the price data into simultaneous views of price break charts, Kagi charts, point and figure charts, and Renko charts, the trader has the ability to see alerts of key locations or landmarks.

Let's explore several examples, starting with the EURUSD. The data is collected and converted into a raw price data file. This can be a live feed or uploaded by the trader. Then the trader can highlight a specific data point on the raw price data file. The highlighted data point will appear over price break charts, Kagi charts, Renko charts,

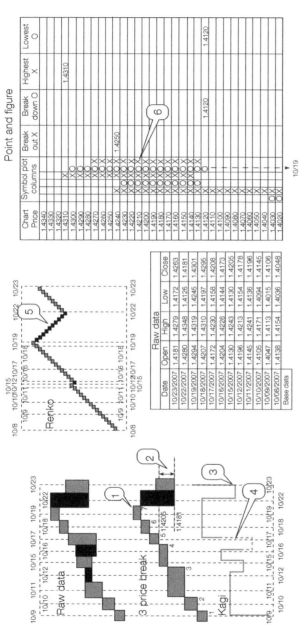

Point and figure

Figure 11.8 Euro Currency Price Matrix Map
Source: Abe Cofnas and Sridhar Iyer

1. Projected Price Break Reversal at 1.4205
2. Distance Beyond Breakpoint to Low Close = 0.0024
3. Forms Waist Support 1.4181
4. Waist Price Turning Point 1.4173
5. Downward Trend from 10/19 to 10/22
6. 3 Price Break Projects Price Reversal in Point & Figure Downtrend Here

Raw data

Date	Open	High	Low	Close
10/23/2007	1.4181	1.4279	1.4172	1.4263
10/22/2007	1.4280	1.4348	1.4126	1.4181
10/19/2007	1.4294	1.4319	1.4245	1.4301
10/18/2007	1.4207	1.4310	1.4197	1.4295
10/17/2007	1.4172	1.4230	1.4158	1.4208
10/16/2007	1.4204	1.4226	1.4144	1.4173
10/15/2007	1.4130	1.4243	1.4130	1.4205
10/12/2007	1.4196	1.4213	1.4154	1.4178
10/11/2007	1.4145	1.4241	1.4136	1.4196
10/10/2007	1.4105	1.4171	1.4094	1.4145
10/09/2007	1.4047	1.4113	1.4015	1.4106
10/08/2007	1.4138	1.4154	1.4036	1.4048
Base data				

and point and figure charts. In effect, the trader obtains a visualization of the price point from four different perspectives simultaneously. The key question is whether each chart type generates price points or landmarks that provide information for the trader. Are there similar projections of support or resistance? Is the price break chart point projected related to a Kagi chart's Yin-to-Yang or Yang-to-Yin turning point? Are Renko chart bricks in an up or down sequence? Does this coincide with the intended direction of the trader? Is the point and figure chart showing a bullish or bearish column? The Price Landmark Matrix provides an instant view by generating a map of the key projections of each chart type.

Let's follow a coordinated path through some Price Landmark Matrix Map examples.

EURUSD

In the EURUSD example in Figure 11.8, let's choose a sample date: October 19, 2007. The first step in navigating the Price Landmark Map is to locate the price break chart. This is a logical first step because price break chart projections are the easiest type to locate. In addition, of all of the alternative charting tools, only price break charts unambiguously project next reversal points. On October 19, the EURUSD was in its seventh consecutive day high. Using the logic that projects the next reversal point, we can count back three lines and see that the chart projected 1.4205 as a break of support resulting in a reversal. On October 23, the reversal actually occurred. At the same time, the Renko chart showed that the black bricks started a series down. This added confirmation that the negative sentiment was in control. The Kagi chart formed a supportive Kagi waist on October 22 at 1.4181. The point and figure chart confirmed that the bullish sentiment was still dominant on October 19 because of the presence of an X column. We can see that Renko charts and point and figure charts acted to confirm the direction, while price break charts and Kagi charts acted to pinpoint the entry areas. If the trader had intentions to sell the EURUSD, the other charts confirmed them. Additionally, the trader could shape a leg-in strategy with an open sell stop order right below the projected price break chart reversal point, with another sell leg when the price broke the Kagi chart waist. A shift in Renko charts on October 23, with three white bricks up, provided a basis for getting out.

This sample is only one example of the functionality of the Price Landmark Matrix. In the Web-based version, it allows a click on any price history point to generate the four-chart visual path.

Gold Price Landmark Matrix

Gold traders can view price action from alternative charting displayed in the Price Landmark Matrix. We can see the results in **Figure 11.9**, a sample extract from the raw price data table before the matrix's algorithms convert it into price break, Kagi, Renko, and point and figure landmarks.

The first chart type is price break charts. The input section provides the user with an opportunity to input settings, and the process section assists programmers in converting the data into price break charts (**Figure 11.10**).

The gold Price Landmark Map section (**Figure 11.11**) provides the key categories that enable a quantitative analysis of the price break patterns.

[GOLD RPD] RAW PRICE DATA				
Date	Open	High	Low	Close
1/23/2009	856.95	903.34	852.99	899.75
1/22/2009	854.30	863.11	844.14	857.00
1/21/2009	857.30	864.66	843.96	854.25
1/20/2009	835.95	866.76	824.19	857.25
1/19/2009	843.99	846.55	832.45	835.90
1/16/2009	817.85	843.65	816.15	843.15
1/15/2009	811.65	821.65	802.59	817.80
1/14/2009	821.95	829.40	807.63	811.70
1/13/2009	820.70	830.40	814.66	822.00
1/12/2009	854.74	857.00	815.93	820.85
1/9/2009	857.50	868.85	845.24	854.20
1/8/2009	842.85	864.59	836.85	857.40

Figure 11.9 Gold Raw Price Data
Source: Bloomberg

[PB IS] INPUT SECTION		[PB PS] PROCESS SECTION (For Programmers)					
[PB NPB] Number of Price 3 Breaks (default 3)							[PB BID] Price Break Box ID
[PB GOLD] Raw Data							
[PB D] Date	[PB C] Close	[PB PM] Price Movement	[PB 3PBR] 3 Price Break Reversal?	[PB BLC] Box Low Close	[PB BHC] Box High Close	[PB BID] Price Break Box ID	
1/23/2009	899.75	Up	Yes	820.85	899.75	Box4	
1/22/2009	857.00	Up	No	820.85	857.00		
1/21/2009	854.25	Down		854.25	857.25		
1/20/2009	857.25	Up	No	820.85	857.25		
1/19/2009	835.90	Down		835.90	843.15		
1/16/2009	843.15	Up	No	820.85	843.15		
1/15/2009	817.80	Up	No	811.70	817.80		
1/14/2009	811.70	Down		811.70	820.85	Box3	
1/13/2009	822.00	Up	No	820.85	822.00		
1/12/2009	820.85	Down		820.85	854.20	Box2	
1/9/2009	854.20	Down		854.20	857.40	Box1	
1/8/2009	857.40						
Base Close							

Figure 11.10 Price Break Input and Process Sections
Source: Bloomberg

The same raw price data can be converted into a data matrix that generates landmarks for Kagi charts on gold **(Figure 11.12)**.

The Renko matrix **(Figure 11.13)** and the point and figure landmark matrix **(Figure 11.14)** provide instant generation of Renko- and point and figure-related data.

All parts of the Price Landmark Matrix's data are then transposed and integrated into the Price Landmark Map, which illustrates in one display key points of price reversal, support, and resistance from the different chart views. For example, the gold price break chart **(Figure 11.5)**

[PB PLM] PRICE LANDMARK MAP SECTION

[PB BID] Price Break Box ID	[PB CHL] Completed Number of Consecutive Highs/Lows	[PB NRP] Next Reversal Price	[PB H] # of Consecutive Highs	[PB L] # of Consecutive Lows	[PB RES] Recommended Entry Strategy	[PB BLC] Distance Beyond Breakpoint To Low Close	[PB BHC] Distance Beyond Breakpoint To High Close	[PB ABLC] Average of the Distance Beyond Breakpoint To Low Close	[PB ABHC] Average of the Distance Beyond Breakpoint To High Close	[PB UR] # Up Reversals From Start Date	[PB DR] # Down Reversals From Start Date	[PB HCUR] Average Sequence of Consecutive High Closes in Up Reversal	[PB DCDR] Average Sequence of Consecutive Down Closes in Down Reversal
Box4	1H		1				42.35		42.35		1		3
Box3	3L	857.40		3	Buy on break above 857.40								
Box2	2L			2									
Box1	1L			1									

Figure 11.11 Gold Price Landmark Map Section

Source: Bloomberg

201

[K PS] PROCESS SECTION (For Programmers)

[K IS] INPUT SECTION

[K PRA] Fixed Percentage Reversal Amount	0.1
[K DAS] Distance above Shoulder(High) in bps	5
[K DBW] Distance below Waist(Low) in bps	5

[K PLM] PRICE LANDMARK MAP SECTION

[K D] Date	[K GOLD] Raw Data [K C] Close	[K LTP] Line Tip Price	[K RALT] Reversal Amount At Line Tip	[K TPL] Turnaround Price Decision at Line Tip [K L] Low	[K H] High	[K CL] Classification [K YIN] Yin	[K YANG] Yang	[K NC] Number of Consecutive [K S] Shoulder/High	[K W] Waist/Low	[K SPTP] Shoulder Price Turning Point	[K PBS] Projected Buy Signal (Yin to Yang)	[K WPTP] Waist Price Turning Point	[K PSS] Projected Sell Signal (Yang to Yin)	[K RYY] Ratio of Yin Length over Yang Length
1/23/2009	899.75	899.75	0.89975	898.85	900.65		Up							
1/22/2009	857.00	857.00	0.857	856.14	857.86		Up		4			854.25		
1/21/2009	854.25	854.25	0.85425	853.40	855.10	Down		3		857.25	843.15			51.42%
1/20/2009	857.25	857.25	0.85725	856.39	858.11		Up		3			835.90		
1/19/2009	835.90	835.90	0.8359	835.06	836.74	Down		2		843.15				

202

1/16/2009	843.15	843.15	0.84315	842.31	843.99	Up			
1/15/2009	817.80	817.80	0.8178	816.98	818.62	Up	2		811.70
1/14/2009	811.70	811.70	0.8117	810.89	812.51	Down	1	822.00	
1/13/2009	822.00	822.00	0.822	821.18	822.82	Up	1		820.85
1/12/2009	820.85	820.85	0.82085	820.03	821.67	Down			
1/9/2009	854.20	854.20	0.8542	853.35	855.05	Down			
1/8/2009	857.40	857.40	0.8574	856.54	858.26				

Base Close

Figure 11.12 Gold: Kagi Price Landmark Matrix

Source: Bloomberg

[R IS] INPUT SECTION		[R PS] PROCESS SECTION (For Programmers)				[R PLM] PRICE LANDMARK MAP SECTION				
[R BS] Brick Setting in bps	25000	[R IC] Intraday Calculations								
[R GOLD] Raw Data										
[R D] Date	[R C] Close	[R BIS] # Bricks in Sequence	[R BC] Brick Color	[R NBB] Next Black Brick	[R NGB] Next Grey Brick	[R DCD] Display Chart Details	[R BM] # Bricks per Time Unit (Brick Momentum)	[R BC] Brick Color	[R NSB] Next Support Breakpoint	[R NRB] Next Resistance Breakpoint
1/2320/09	899.75	17	Grey	894.90	897.40	1/23/09	17	Grey	7	Grey
1/22/2009	857.00	0		852.40	854.90					
1/21/2009	854.25	0		852.40	854.90					
1/2020/09	857.25	6	Grey	852.40	854.90	1/20/09	6	Grey	2	Black
1/19/2009	835.90	1	Black	837.40	839.90	1/19/09	1	Black	12	Grey
1/16/2009	843.15	10	Grey	839.90	842.40	1/16/2009	11	Grey	19	Black
1/15/2009	817.80	1	Grey	814.90	817.40					
1/14/2009	811.70	4	Black	812.40	814.90	1/14/2009	18	Black		
1/13/2009	822.00	0		822.40	824.90					
1/12/2009	820.85	13	Black	822.40	824.90					
1/9/2009	854.20	1	Black	854.90	857.40					
1/8/2009	857.40	0		857.40	857.40	1/8/2009				
Base Close										

Figure 11.13 Gold: Renko Price Landmark Matrix

Source: Bloomberg

[PAF IS] INPUT SECTION — **[PAF PS] PROCESS SECTION (For Programmers)** — **[PAF PLM] PRICE LANDMARK MAP SECTION**

[PAF BS] Box Size (in bps): **10**
[PAF BRR] # Box Reversals Required To Change Column: **3**

[PAF GOLD] Raw Data and Process Section:

[PAF D] Date	[PAF H] High	[PAF L] Low	[PAF TF] Trend Flag	[PAF NUV] Next Uptrend Value OR BoxCeiling(ParentHigh)	[PAF BFH] BoxFloor(High)	[PAF NDV] Next Downtrend Value or BoxFloor(ParentLow)	[PAF BCL] BoxCeiling(Low)	[PAF LP] Last Plot	[PAF PR] High	[PAF PR] Low	[PAF SC] Symbol Count	[PAF PS] Plot Symbol	[PAF CN] Column Number
1/23/09	903.34	852.99	Uptrend	870.00	900.00			900.00		870.00	4	X	2
1/22/09	863.11	844.14	No Trend										
1/21/09	864.66	843.96	No Trend										
1/20/09	866.76	824.19	Uptrend	850.00	860.00			860.00		830.00	2	X	2
1/19/09	846.55	832.45	No Trend										
1/16/09	843.65	816.15	Uptrend	820.00	840.00			840.00		810.00	3	X	2
1/15/09	821.65	802.59	No Trend										
1/14/09	829.40	807.63	Downtrend			810.00	810.00	840.00			1	O	1
1/13/09	830.40	814.66	No Trend					810.00					
1/12/09	857.00	815.93	Downtrend			830.00	820.00	850.00			2	O	1
1/9/09	868.85	845.24	No Trend										
1/8/09	864.59	836.85	No Trend										

Base

[PAF PLM] Price Landmark Map Section:

[PAF CP] Chart Price	[PAF SPC] Symbol Plot Columns 1	[PAF SPC] Symbol Plot Columns 2	[PAF BX] Breakout X	[PAF BO] Breakdown O	[PAF HX] Highest X	[PAF LO] Lowest O
900		X			900.00	
890		X				
880		X				
870		X				
860		X				
850		X				
840		X				
830	O	X				
820	O	X				
810	O					810.00

Figure 11.14 Gold: Point and Figure Price Landmark Matrix

Source: Bloomberg

Raw data

Date	Open	High	Low	Close
1/23/2009	856.95	903.34	852.99	899.75
1/22/2009	854.30	863.11	844.14	857.00
1/21/2009	857.30	864.66	843.96	854.25
1/20/2009	835.95	866.76	824.19	857.25
1/19/2009	843.99	846.55	832.45	835.90
1/16/2009	817.85	843.65	816.15	843.15
1/15/2009	811.65	821.65	802.59	817.80
1/14/2009	821.95	829.40	807.63	811.70
1/13/2009	820.70	830.40	814.66	822.00
1/12/2009	854.74	857.00	815.93	820.85
1/09/2009	857.50	868.85	845.24	854.20
1/08/2009	842.85	864.59	836.85	857.40

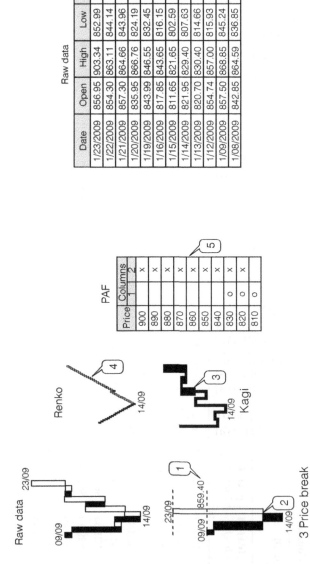

Renko

Kagi

Raw data

3 Price break

PAF

1. Between 9/22 and 9/23
2. Projected price break reversal at 857.40
3. Yang on 9/20
4. Renko uptrend matches with 3 Price Break
5. Price break projects price reversal in point & figure uptrend here

Figure 11.15 Gold Price Landmark Map

Source: Abe Cofnas and Sridhar Iyer

projected an upward price reversal at 857.40 on January 14, 2009. On
January 20, 2009, the Kagi chart showed the Yin turning to a Yang at the
same price point. At the same time, the point and figure chart reversed
columns from an X to an O. Finally, Renko bricks were in a consistent
uptrend. All four charts provided landmarks that confirmed a bullish
reversal in gold.

Crude Oil

Crude oil price action in the Price Landmark Matrix is synthesized via
a similar path. **Figures 11.16** and **11.17** show that there is an input
section with the raw price data; a process section that converts the data
into important categories for programming; and a price landmark map
section, which displays the price break, Kagi, Renko, and point and
figure elements of the data.

In the crude oil Price Landmark Map (**Figure 11.18**), as in the
other maps, the trader starts with the price break reversal projection
and then looks for confirming landmark alerts from the Kagi and
Renko charts. In the sample map, we see that on December 24,
2008 the crude oil price reversal point was projected to be at 49.52.
A trader intending to shape a long position would therefore consider
that price point as a key one for entry. An open buy stop order above
this point would be justified, and would be triggered when the price
reversal column went through it. Another tactic would be to enter on
a market order. Kagi charts revealed that the same price break point
at 49.52 was a waist formation, which indicates support. This occurred
on December 18, 2008, before the price break projection. This is an
example of confluence. In trading terms, the price break reversal going
through a Kagi waist is similar to a bounce of support. The Kagi chart
also showed a shift in sentiment on December 29, 2008 at 47.46, when
the Yin turned to a Yang. In this case, the Kagi chart presented a buy
signal before the price break projection point. The trader can be a bit
aggressive and put on a market order at this Yin-to-Yang conversion.
Looking at the Renko bricks, they actually went into a bullish sequence
on December 24, reversing a sequence of ten bricks down. Finally,
the point and figure chart was still in an O column when the bullish
price reversal actually occurred. An X column didn't appear until
December 29. In the crude oil example, price break, Kagi, and point
and figure worked to confirm the bullish entry strategy.

[PB IS] INPUT SECTION		[PB PS] PROCESS SECTION (For Programmers)					
[PB NPB] Number of Price Breaks (default 3)		3					
[PB OIL] Raw Data		[PB PM] Price Movement	[PB 3PBR] 3 Price Break Reversal?	[PB BLC] Box Low Close	[PB BHC] Box High Close	[PB BID] Price Break Box ID
[PB D] Date	[PB C] Close					
1/2/2009	54.73	Up	Yes	53.16	54.73	Box7
12/31/2008	53.16	Up	Yes	46.52	53.16	Box6
12/30/2008	47.67	Up	No	47.46	47.67	
12/29/2008	47.46	Up	No	45.08	47.46	
12/26/2008	45.08	Up	No	42.79	45.08	
12/24/2008	42.79	Down		42.79	46.52	Box5
12/23/2008	46.52	Down		46.52	47.46	Box4
12/22/2008	47.46	Down		47.46	49.52	Box3
12/19/2008	50.05	Up	No	49.52	50.05	
12/18/2008	49.52	Down		49.52	51.86	Box2
12/17/2008	51.86	Down		51.86	53.10	Box1
12/16/2008	53.10					
Base Close						

Figure 11.16 Crude Oil Price Landmark Matrix: Input and Process Sections
Source: Bloomberg

The DAX and the Price Landmark Matrix

The DAX is an important index in global markets, as it tracks thirty German blue-chip stocks. We applied the Price Landmark Matrix to the sample of data presented in **Figures 11.19** through **11.22.**

The Price Landmark Matrix generated an integrated map that projected, on October 31, 2008, a price reversal location at 4869.30, which was reached on November 4. Notice that the Kagi chart had formed a shoulder a few days earlier, on October 28, at 4823.45. This meant that a trader would not want to enter on the price reversal projected.

[PB PLM]
PRICE LANDMARK MAP SECTION

[PB CHL] Completed Number of Consecutive Highs/Lows	[PB NRP] Next Reversal Price	[PB H] # of Consecutive Highs	[PB L] # of Consecutive Lows	[PB RES] Recommended Entry Strategy	[PB BLC] Distance Beyond Breakpoint To Low Close	[PB BHC] Distance Beyond Breakpoint To High Close	[PB ABLC] Average of the Distance Beyond Breakpoint To Low Close	[PB ABHC] Average of the Distance Beyond Breakpoint To High Close	[PB UR] # Up Reversals From Start Date	[PB DR] # Down Reversals From Start Date	[PB HCUR] Average Sequence of Consecutive High Closes in Up Reversal	[PB DCDR] Average Sequence of Consecutive Down Closes in Down Reversal
2H		2				5.21		4.42		5		5
1H		1				3.64		3.64		5		5
5L	49.52		5	Buy on break above 49.52								
4L	51.86		4	Buy on break above 51.86								
3L	53.10		3	Buy on break above 53.10								
2L			2									
1L			1									

Figure 11.17 Crude Oil Price Landmark Matrix: Price Landmark Map Section

Source: Bloomberg

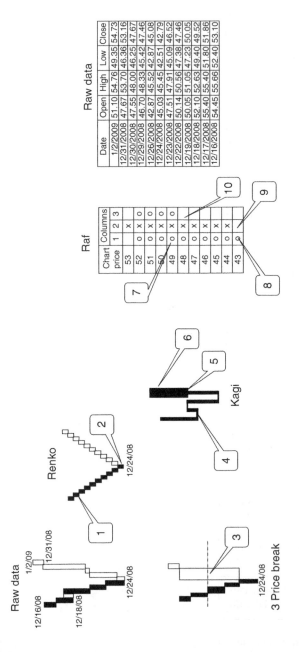

Raw data

Date	Open	High	Low	Close
1/2/2009	51.10	54.76	49.35	54.73
12/31/2008	47.67	53.70	46.36	53.16
12/30/2008	47.55	48.00	46.25	47.67
12/29/2008	46.70	48.33	45.42	47.46
12/26/2008	42.87	45.52	42.87	45.08
12/24/2008	45.03	45.45	42.51	42.79
12/23/2008	47.51	47.91	45.09	46.52
12/22/2008	50.14	50.56	47.38	47.46
12/19/2008	50.05	51.05	47.23	50.05
12/18/2008	52.10	52.63	49.40	49.52
12/17/2008	55.40	55.40	51.80	51.86
12/16/2008	54.45	55.66	52.40	53.10

Raf

Chart price	Columns 1	2	3
53		x	
52	o	x	o
51	o	x	o
50	o	x	o
49	o	x	
48	o	x	
47	o	x	
46	o	x	
45	o	x	
44	o	x	
43	o	o	

Renko

Raw data

12/16/08
1/2/09
12/31/08
12/18/08
12/24/08

12/24/08

Kagi

3 Price break

12/24/08

1. Second black brick corresponds to projected reversal
   Price 49.52
2. 10 Renko black bricks downtrend ends on 12/24/09
3. Reversal price projected is 49.52
4. Waist 49.52 occurred on 12/18/08
5. Yang began on 12/29/08 at 47.46, which equals first
   shoulder
6. Projected reversal price of 49.52 in yang region between
   12/30/08 and 12/31/08
7. Projected reversal price (49.52) occurs between
   12/22/08 and 12/23/08
8. Column 1 between 12/17/08–12/24/08
9. Column 2 between 12/29/08–12/31/08
10. Column 3 corresponds to 1/2/09

Figure 11.18 Oil Price Landmark Map

Source: Abe Cofnas and Sridhar Iyer

210

[DAX RPD] RAW PRICE DATA				
Date	Open	High	Low	Close
11/6/2008	5101.98	5101.98	4781.51	4813.57
11/5/2008	5268.80	5271.91	5142.85	5166.87
11/4/2008	5018.83	5302.57	4993.10	5278.04
11/3/2008	5053.94	5089.54	4967.94	5026.84
10/31/2008	4856.02	5066.81	4785.11	4987.97
10/30/2008	4894.14	5042.49	4827.27	4869.30
10/29/2008	4460.26	4885.85	4460.26	4808.69
10/28/2008	4314.91	4823.45	4314.91	4823.45
10/27/2008	4143.45	4486.13	4062.77	4334.64
10/24/2008	4362.79	4362.93	4014.60	4295.67
10/23/2008	4559.71	4576.87	4364.20	4519.70
10/22/2008	4739.74	4740.31	4535.64	4571.07
Base Data				

Figure 11.19 DAX Raw Price Data
Source: Bloomberg

If the reversal were below the shoulder, it would be stronger. Renko bricks turned black on November 5, which was after the price break. Accordingly, a trader could use the Renko chart to add a position if he had already entered it. The point and figure was still an X column on November 4, but it turned to O on November 5, offering confirmation to enter a short.

S&P 500 and the Price Landmark Matrix

How would we trade the S&P 500 index with the assistance of alternative charting signals? Let's look at a Price Landmark Matrix with sample S&P 500 data. We begin by entering the raw price data (**Figure 11.23**). The raw data is converted into signals for each alternative chart. There are separate matrices for price break (**Figures 11.24–11.25**); Kagi (**Figure 11.26** and **11.27**); Renko (**Figure 11.28**); and point and figure (**Figure 11.29**) charts.

[PB IS] INPUT SECTION			[PB PS] PROCESS SECTION (For Programmers)			
[PB NPB] Number of Price Breaks (default 3)		3				
[PB DAX] Raw Data		[PB PM] Price Movement	[PB 3PBR] 3 Price Break Reversal?	[PB BLC] Box Low Close	[PB BHC] Box High Close	[PB BID] Price Break Box ID
[PB D] Date	[PB C] Close					
11/6/2008	4813.57	Down	Yes	4813.57	5026.84	Box8
11/5/2008	5166.87	Down	No	5166.87	5026.84	
11/4/2008	5278.04	Up		5026.84	5278.04	Box7
11/3/2008	5026.84	Up		4987.97	5026.84	Box6
10/31/2008	4987.97	Up		4869.30	4987.97	Box5
10/30/2008	4869.30	Up		4823.45	4869.30	Box4
10/29/2008	4808.69	Down	No	4808.69	4823.45	
10/28/2008	4823.45	Up	No	4295.67	4823.45	Box3
10/27/2008	4334.64	Up	No	4295.67	4334.64	
10/24/2008	4295.67	Down		4295.67	4519.70	Box2
10/23/2008	4519.70	Down		4519.70	4571.07	Box1
10/22/2007	4571.07					
Base Close						

Figure 11.20 DAX Price Break Input and Process Sections
Source: Bloomberg

The SPX Price Landmark Map

Using the Price Landmark concept for SPX (**Figures 11.23–11.32**), we begin by noticing that the price break issued a reversal projection at 1260.32 on July 23, 2008. There are many Kagi shoulder turns near that date, indicating that the price was not stable here. Importantly, Kagi formed a shoulder at 1257.16 on July 28. This shoulder is below the projected reversal point. Since shoulders form a resistance, we see that

[PB PLM] PRICE LANDMARK MAP SECTION

[PB CHL] Completed Number of Consecutive Highs/Lows	[PB NRP] Next Reversal Price	[PB H] # of Consecutive Highs	[PB L] # of Consecutive Lows	[PB RES] Recommended Entry Strategy	[PB BLC] Distance Beyond Breakpoint To Low Close	[PB BHC] Distance Beyond Breakpoint To High Close	[PB ABLC] Average of the Distance Beyond Breakpoint To Low Close	[PB ABHC] Average of the Distance Beyond Breakpoint To High Close	[PB UR] # Up Reversals From Start Date	[PB DR] # Down Reversals From Start Date	[PB HCUR] Average Sequence of Consecutive High Closes in Up Reversal	[PB DCDR] Average Sequence of Consecutive Down Closes in Down Reversal
1L			1		55.73		55.73		1		5	
5H	4869.30	5		Sell on break below 4869.30								
4H	4823.45	4		Sell on break below 4823.45								
3H	4295.67	3		Sell on break below 4295.67								
2H		2										
1H		1										
2L			2									
1L			1									

Figure 11.21 DAX Price Landmark Matrix Map Section

Source: Bloomberg

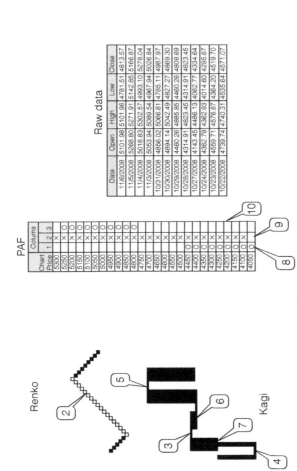

Raw data

Renko

Kagi

3 Price break

PAF

	Colums		
Chart Price	1	2	3
5300	×		
5250	×	○	
5200	×	○	
5150	×	○	
5100	×	○	
5050	×	○	
5000	×	○	
4950	×	○	
4900	×	○	○
4850	×	○	○
4800	×	○	○
4750	×		
4700	×		
4650	×		
4600	×		
4550	×		
4500	×		
4450	○	×	
4400	○	×	
4350	○	×	
4300	○	×	
4250	○	×	
4200	○	×	
4150	○	×	
4100	○	×	
4050	○		

Raw data

Date	Open	High	Low	Close
11/6/2008	5101.98	5101.98	4781.51	4813.57
11/5/2008	5268.80	5271.91	5142.85	5166.87
11/4/2008	5018.83	5302.57	4993.10	5278.04
11/3/2008	5053.94	5089.54	4967.94	5026.84
10/31/2008	4856.02	5066.81	4785.11	4997.97
10/30/2008	4894.14	5042.49	4827.27	4969.30
10/29/2008	4460.26	4885.85	4460.26	4808.69
10/28/2008	4314.91	4823.45	4314.91	4823.45
10/27/2008	4143.45	4486.13	4062.77	4334.64
10/24/2008	4382.79	4362.93	4014.60	4295.67
10/23/2008	4559.71	4576.87	4364.20	4519.70
10/22/2008	4739.74	4740.31	4535.64	4571.07

1. Reversal Price Projected is 4869.30
2. Reversal price projected on 11/4/08 is same as on or after the 13th Grey brick
3. Shoulder 1 on 10/28/08 equals 4823.45
4. Waist 1 on 10/24/08 equals 4295.67
5. Shoulder 2 on 11/4/08 equals 5278.04

6. Waist 2 on 10/29/08 equals 4823.45
7. Yang begins between 10/27/08–10/28/08 and equals 4571.07
8. Column 1 between 10/22/08–10/24/08
9. Column 2 between 10/27/08–11/4/08
10. Column 3 between 11/5/08–11/6/08

Figure 11.22 DAX Price Landmark Map

Source: Abe Cofnas and Sridhar Iyer

214

[SPX RPD] RAW PRICE DATA				
Date	Open	High	Low	Close
7/28/2008	1257.76	1260.09	1234.37	1234.37
7/25/2008	1253.51	1263.23	1251.75	1257.76
7/24/2008	1283.22	1283.22	1251.48	1252.54
7/23/2008	1278.87	1291.17	1276.06	1282.19
7/22/2008	1257.08	1277.42	1248.83	1277.00
7/21/2008	1261.82	1267.74	1255.70	1260.00
7/18/2008	1258.22	1262.23	1251.81	1260.68
7/17/2008	1246.31	1262.31	1241.49	1260.32
7/16/2008	1214.65	1245.52	1211.39	1245.36
7/15/2008	1226.83	1234.35	1200.44	1214.91
7/14/2008	1241.61	1253.50	1225.01	1228.30
7/11/2008	1248.66	1257.27	1225.35	1239.49
Base Data				

Figure 11.23 S&P 500 Raw Price Data
Source: Bloomberg

the price break reversal down was below the price break reversal point. The trader needs to wait for a sell signal: a Yang turning to a Yin. This occurred on July 25 at 1252.64. Renko charts started the downturn on July 24. The point and figure chart shows the formation of an O column between July 24and July 28.

Conclusion on the Price Landmark Matrix

We can make several important points about the best way to integrate price break, Kagi, point and figure, and Renko charts. First, price break charts are the best logical point to initiate the analysis. This is because price break charts are the only ones that project reversal points and where they will be. This means that Kagi charts, point and figure charts, and Renko bricks act as confirming coincident indicators. Traders will vary how much weight to give each chart's signals, depending on their

[PB IS] INPUT SECTION		[PB PS] PROCESS SECTION (For Programmers)				
[PB NPB] Number of Price Breaks (default 3)	3					
[PB SPX] Raw Data		[PB PM] Price Movement	[PB 3PBR] 3 Price Break Reversal?	[PB BLC] Box Low Close	[PB BHC] Box High Close	[PB BID] Price Break Box ID
[PB D] Date	[PB C] Close					
7/28/2008	1234.37	Down	Yes	1234.37	1252.54	Box9
7/25/2008	1257.76	Up		1252.54	1257.76	
7/24/2008	1252.54	Down	Yes	1252.54	1277.00	Box8
7/23/2008	1282.19	Up		1277.00	1282.19	Box7
7/22/2008	1277.00	Up		1260.68	1277.00	Box6
7/21/2008	1260.00	Down	No	1260.00	1260.68	
7/18/2008	1260.68	Up		1260.32	1260.68	Box5
7/17/2008	1260.32	Up		1245.36	1260.32	Box4
7/16/2008	1245.36	Up		1228.30	1245.36	Box3
7/15/2008	1214.91	Down		1214.91	1228.30	Box2
7/14/2008	1228.30	Down		1228.30	1239.49	Box1
7/11/2008	1239.49					

Base Close

Figure 11.24 S&P 500: Price Break Process Section
Source: Bloomberg

own strategies. Position traders looking for setups and swings will concentrate on price break chart projected reversals. Those traders looking for intraday momentum signals can look to Kagi, point and figure, and Renko charts.

The examples in this chapter only show one price point. In the Web-based version, the trader can click on any point and see its

[PB PLM] PRICE LANDMARK MAP SECTION

[PB CHL] Completed Number of Consecutive Highs/Lows	[PB NRP] Next Reversal Price	[PB H] # of Consecutive Highs	[PB L] # of Consecutive Lows	[PB RES] Recommended Entry Strategy	[PB BLC] Distance Beyond Breakpoint To Low Close	[PB BHC] Distance Beyond Breakpoint To High Close	[PB ABLC] Average of the Distance Beyond Breakpoint To Low Close	[PB ABHC] Average of the Distance Beyond Break-point To High Close	[PB UR] # Up Reversals From Start Date	[PB DR] # Down Reversals From Start Date	[PB HCUR] Average Sequence of Consecutive High Closes in Up Reversal	[PB DCDR] Average Sequence of Consecutive Down Closes in Down Reversal
2L			2		25.95		16.87		1		5	
1L			1		7.78		7.78		1		5	
5H	1260.32	5		Sell on break below 1260.32								
4H	1245.36	4		Sell on break below 1245.36								
3H	1228.30	3		Sell on break below 1228.30								
2H		2										
1H		1										
2L			2									
1L			1									

Figure 11.25 S&P 500: Price Break Price Landmark Map Section

Source: Bloomberg

[K IS] INPUT SECTION	[K PS] PROCESS SECTION (For Programmers)				
[K PRA] Fixed Percentage Reversal Amount					0.1
[K DAS] Distance above Shoulder(High) in bps					5
[K DBW] Distance below Waist(Low) in bps					5
[K SPX] Raw Data		[K LTP] Line Tip Price	[K RALT] Reversal Amount At Line Tip	[K TPL] Turnaround Price Decision at Line Tip	
[K D] Date	[K C] Close			[K L] Low	[K H] High
7/28/2008	1234.37	1234.37	1.2343700	1233.14	1235.60
7/25/2008	1257.76	1257.76	1.2577600	1256.50	1259.02
7/24/2008	1252.54	1252.54	1.2525400	1251.29	1253.79
7/23/2008	1282.19	1282.19	1.2821900	1280.91	1283.47
7/22/2008	1277.00	1277.00	1.2770000	1275.72	1278.28
7/21/2008	1260.00	1260.00	1.2600000	1258.74	1261.26
7/18/2008	1260.68	1260.68	1.2606800	1259.42	1261.94
7/17/2008	1260.32	1260.32	1.2603200	1259.06	1261.58
7/16/2008	1245.36	1245.36	1.2453600	1244.11	1246.61
7/15/2008	1214.91	1214.91	1.2149100	1213.70	1216.12
7/14/2008	1228.30	1228.30	1.2283000	1227.07	1229.53
7/11/2008	1239.49	1239.49	1.2394900	1238.25	1240.73

Base Close

Figure 11.26 S&P 500: Kagi Input and Process Sections
Source: Bloomberg

[K PLM]
PRICE LANDMARK MAP SECTION

[K CL] Classification		[K NC] Number of Consecutive		[K SPTP] Shoulder Price Turning Point	[K PBS] Projected Buy Signal (Yin to Yang)	[K WPTP] Waist Price Turning Point	[K PSS] Projected Sell Signal (Yang to Yin)	[K RYY] Ratio of Yin Length over Yang Length
[K YIN] Yin	[K YANG] Yang	[K S] Shoulder/ High	[K W] Waist/ Low					
Down		2		1257.76			1252.54	348.08%
	Up		2			1252.54		
	Down	1		1282.19	1239.49			57.56%
	Up							
	Up							
	Up							
	Up		1			1214.91		
Down								
Down								

Figure 11.27 S&P 500: Kagi Price Landmark Map Section

Source: Bloomberg

[R IS] INPUT SECTION			[R PS] PROCESS SECTION (For Programmers)					[R PLM] PRICE LANDMARK MAP SECTION				
Brick Set-ting in bps [R BS] 50000			[R IC] Intraday Calculations					[R DCD] Display Chart Details	[R BM] # Bricks per Time Unit (Brick Momentum)	[R BC] Brick Color	[R NSB] Next Support Breakpoint	[R NRB] Next Resistance Breakpoint
[R SPX] Raw Data		[R BIS] # Bricks in Sequence	[R BC] Brick Color	[R NBB] Next Black Brick	[R NGB] Next Grey Brick							
[R D] Date	[R C] Close											
7/28/2008	1234.37	4	Black	1234.49	1239.49	7/28/2008	4	Black	5 Black	
7/25/2008	1257.76	0		1254.49	1259.49	7/25/2008	0			
7/24/2008	1252.54	4	Black	1254.49	1259.49	7/24/2008	4	Black		5 Grey
7/23/2008	1282.19	1	Grey	1274.49	1279.49	7/23/2008	4	Grey		8 Grey
7/22/2008	1277.00	3	Grey	1269.49	1274.49					
7/21/2008	1260.00	0		1254.49	1259.49	7/21/2008	0			
7/18/2008	1260.68	0		1254.49	1259.49	7/18/2008	0			
7/17/2008	1260.32	3	Grey	1254.49	1259.49	7/17/2008	7	Grey	5 Black	
7/16/2008	1245.36	4	Grey	1239.49	1244.49					
7/15/2008	1214.91	2	Black	1219.49	1224.49	7/15/2008	4	Black		
7/14/2008	1228.30	2	Black	1229.49	1234.49					
7/11/2008	1239.49	0		1239.49	1239.49	7/11/2008				
Base Close										

Figure 11.28 S&P 500: Renko

Source: Bloomberg

[PAF IS] INPUT SECTION		
[PAF BS] **Box Size (in bps)**	10	
[PAF BRR] **# Box Reversals Required To Change Column**	3	
	[PAF SPX] **Raw Data**	
[PAF D] Date	**[PAF H] High**	**[PAF L] Low**
7/28/2008	1260.09	1234.37
7/25/2008	1263.23	1251.75
7/24/2008	1283.22	1251.48
7/23/2008	1291.17	1276.06
7/22/2008	1277.42	1248.83
7/21/2008	1267.74	1255.70
7/18/2008	1262.23	1251.81
7/17/2008	1262.31	1241.49
7/16/2008	1245.52	1211.39
7/15/2008	1234.35	1200.44
7/14/2008	1253.50	1225.01
7/11/2008	1257.27	1225.35
Base		

Figure 11.29 S&P 500: Point and Figure Input Section
Source: Bloomberg

interrelationships within this universe. Moreover, the trader need not search for points in each chart that are important, because they highlight automatically.

The Price Landmark Matrix concept also provides a logical infrastructure for the next generation of "smart" charts and tools. The matrix is programmable to run queries in the background about market conditions and provide alerts on key areas. For example, if a projected reversal

[PAF PS] PROCESS SECTION (For Programmers)										
[PAF TF] Trend Flag	[PAF UP] Uptrend Parameters		[PAF DP] Downtrend Parameters		[PAF LP] Last Plot	[PAF PR] Price Reversal		[PAF SC] Symbol Count	[PAF PS] Plot Symbol	[PAF CN] Column Number
	[PAF NUV] Next Uptrend Value OR BoxCeiling (ParentHigh)	[PAF BFH] BoxFloor(High)	[PAF NDV] Next Downtrend Value OR BoxFloor(ParentLow)	[PAF BCL] BoxCeiling(Low)		[PAF H] High	[PAF L] Low			
Downtrend			1250.00	1240.00	1240.00	1270.00		2	O	3
Downtrend			1280.00	1260.00	1260.00	1290.00		3	O	3
Uptrend	1280.00	1290.00			1290.00		1260.00	2	X	2
Uptrend	1270.00	1270.00			1270.00		1240.00	1	X	2
Uptrend	1260.00	1260.00			1260.00		1230.00	1	X	2
Uptrend	1250.00	1260.00			1260.00		1230.00	2	X	2
Uptrend	1220.00	1240.00			1240.00		1210.00	3	X	2
Downtrend			1220.00	1210.00	1210.00	1240.00		2	O	1

Figure 11.30 S&P 500: Point and Figure Process Section

Source: Bloomberg

[PAF PLM]
PRICE LANDMARK MAP SECTION

[PAF CP] Chart Price	[PAF SPC] Symbol Plot Columns			[PAF BX] Breakout X	[PAF BO] Breakdown O	[PAF HX] Highest X	[PAF LO] Lowest O
	1	2	3				
1290.00		X		1290.00		1290.00	
1280.00		X	O				
1270.00		X	O				
1260.00		X	O				
1250.00		X	O				
1240.00		X	O				
1230.00		X					
1220.00	O	X					
1210.00	O						1210.00

Figure 11.31 S&P 500: Point and Figure Price Landmark Map Section
Source: Bloomberg

in price break data is coincident with a key technical indicator like a moving average or Fibonacci resistance line, the data cell can be highlighted. For Kagi, if the turn from Yin to Yang, or Yang to Yin, coincides with similar indicators, the same application would occur. If a point and figure X or O appeared on a 45-degree line, the trader would be alerted. Finally, if a Renko sequence of blocks were coincident with a Bollinger band, a similar alert would be embedded. The potential for a "smarter" matrix is great.

A question often arises about whether building an integrated price break, Kagi, point and figure, and Renko trading system is a next step. Such a system can be constructed and developed through genetic algorithms (GAs) that actually learn from their mistakes. Back testing is of limited use. A far better approach is "forward testing"—in other

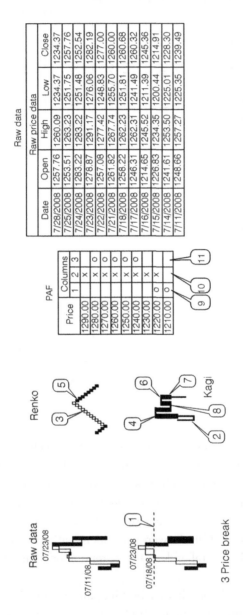

Figure 11.32 S&P 500 Price Landmark Map

Source: Bloomberg

Raw data

Raw price data

Date	Open	High	Low	Close
7/28/2008	1257.76	1260.09	1234.37	1234.37
7/25/2008	1253.51	1263.23	1251.75	1257.76
7/24/2008	1283.22	1283.22	1251.48	1252.54
7/23/2008	1278.87	1291.17	1276.06	1282.19
7/22/2008	1257.08	1277.42	1248.83	1277.00
7/21/2008	1261.82	1267.74	1255.70	1260.00
7/18/2008	1258.22	1262.23	1251.81	1260.68
7/17/2008	1246.31	1262.31	1241.49	1260.32
7/16/2008	1214.65	1245.52	1211.39	1245.36
7/15/2008	1226.83	1234.35	1200.44	1214.91
7/14/2008	1241.61	1253.50	1225.01	1228.30
7/11/2008	1248.66	1257.27	1225.35	1239.49

PAF

Price	Columns 1	2	3
1290.00		x	
1280.00		x	o
1270.00		x	o
1260.00		x	o
1250.00		x	o
1240.00		x	o
1230.00		x	
1220.00	o		
1210.00	o		

Renko

Kagi

Raw data
07/23/08

07/11/08

07/23/08

07/18/08

3 Price break

1. Reversal price projected is 1260.32
2. Waist 1 on 7/16/08 equals 1214.91
3. Reversal price projected on 7/23/08 is on or after 7 gray bricks
4. Shoulder 1 on 7/24/08 equals 1282.19
5. Downtrend starts on 7/24/08
6. Shoulder 2 on 7/28/08 equals 1257.16
7. Yang appears on or after 7/25/08 and is at 1252.54
8. Waist 2 on 7/25/08 equals 1252.54
9. Column 1 between 7/11/08–7/15/08
10. Column 2 between 7/16/08–7/23/08
11. Column 3 between 7/24/08–7/28/08

words, putting on trades under a supervised plan designed to attack specific weaknesses that the plan uncovers. The best approach, however, is not to test forward and produce a system, but instead to produce alerts. Trading alerts make more sense than systems, because an alert is an early warning process that avoids the fatal flaw of any system: its inability to capture all of the variables that influence price. Alerts allow the trader to use human intelligence, which is far more powerful than systems, to spot nuances in changing markets.

CHAPTER 12

New Directions in Sentiment Analysis
Charting Words

THE AIM OF this chapter is to introduce the emerging field of text mining as a new form of sentiment analysis for use in trading markets.

This book has really been about the analysis of the shape of sentiment. We first looked at how traders can apply alternative charting to detect sentiment in the market. We can deduce that a price point in the market, represented by a candlestick, line, bar chart, price break chart, Kagi chart, or Renko chart, is the result of an adversarial contest between buyers and sellers. Each price close represents a unit of sentiment. From this perspective, we can consider technical analysis or chart reading to be a branch of shape science. As a result, a chart type is really a shape that has been revealed from sample data. Accordingly, price break charts, Kagi charts, point and figure charts, and Renko charts represent shapes but use different landmarks. The application of these charts is not very different from any pattern recognition process that cuts across disciplines. We can apply some of the principles of shape analysis, which started with the science of *morphometrics* (the study of biological form), to chart reading.[1]

Consider the following statement: "Shape is a definite entity, a configuration of points that keep geometric relationships among them."[2] Recognizing the shape of surprise in the market is not really different from recognizing a face in a crowd. Seen in this context, charting is a form of shape science.

What is exciting about our current time is that the art and the science of analyzing sentiment in the market are evolving. Charts following this logic do not simply map price action, but also track opinion data. We see this in consumer and producer sentiment data and the charting of that data. Also emerging is a new branch of sentiment analysis that is generating an entirely new type of data for the trader to evaluate and use in shaping trades. We are referring to the field of "text mining." The field involves *information extraction* (IE), *natural language processing* (NLP), *text mining*, and *event analysis*. Economists at the Federal Reserve have recognized the need for real-time data sets that enable the gathering of information about economic conditions that is more precise than that currently available. A recent research report stated:

> Aggregate business conditions are of central importance in the business, finance, and policy communities worldwide, and huge resources are devoted to assessment of the continuously evolving state of the real economy. Literally thousands of newspapers, newsletters, television shows, and blogs, not to mention armies of employees in manufacturing and service industries, including the financial services industries, central banks, government and nongovernment organizations, grapple constantly with the measurement and fore-casting of evolving business conditions. Of central importance is the constant grappling. Real economic agents, making real decisions, in real time, want accurate and timely estimates of the state of real activity. Business cycle chronologies such as those of the [National Bureau of Economic Research], which proclaim expansions and contractions long after the fact, are not useful in that regard.[3]

In this report's conclusion, there is an explicit recognition of the importance of words. Here is what the authors say:

> We look forward to … [i]ncorporation of indicators beyond macroeconomic and financial data. In particular, it will be of interest to attempt inclusion of qualitative information such as headline news.[4]

The Federal Reserve Bank of Philadelphia has established the "Real-Time Data Research Center." Research there focuses on how to involve real-time data such as business forecasts in tracking economic conditions, as well as separating "the signal from the noise."

This focus is profoundly important because as a result, real-time, high-frequency surveys of "opinion" will produce new information for traders to consider. A recent study noted the importance of this category of new research:

> Traders in financial markets are confronted with the problem that too much information is available from various, heterogeneous sources like newswires, forums, blogs, and collaborative tools. In order to make accurate trading decisions, traders have to filter the relevant information efficiently so that they are able to react to new information in a timely manner.[5] This field is new, but is rapidly developing a topology and logic for the construction of technical tools. The figure below shows the overall logic.

Of course, we are interested in the application of "text mining" to trading. A recent study in the field of computational intelligence focused on the application to stock prediction states:

> Mining textual documents and time series concurrently, such as predicting the movements of stock prices based on news articles, is an emerging topic in data mining society nowadays. Previous research has already suggested that the relationships between news articles and stock prices do exist. However, all of the existing approaches are concerning mining single time series only. The interrelationships among different stocks are not well addressed. Mining multiple time series concurrently is not only more informative but also far more challenging. Research in such a direction is lacking. In this paper, we try to explore such an opportunity and propose a systematic framework for mining multiple time series based on the Efficient Market Hypothesis.[6]

A recent article released by the Federal Reserve and focused on the impact of words states,

> The Federal Reserve's announcement following its January 28, 2004, policy meeting led to one of the largest reactions in the Treasury market on record, with two- and five-year yields jumping 20 and 25 basis points (bp) respectively in the half-hour

surrounding the announcement—the largest movements around any Federal Open Market Committee (FOMC) announcement over the fourteen years for which we have data. "We find that 75 to 90 percent of the explainable variation in five- and ten-year Treasury yields in response to monetary policy announcements is due to the path factor (associated with statements) rather than to changes in the federal funds rate target." ... The study concluded, "Do central bank actions speak louder than words? We find that the answer to this question is a qualified "no." In particular, we find that viewing the effects of FOMC announcements on financial markets as driven by a single factor—changes in the federal funds rate target—is inadequate. Instead, we find that a second policy factor—one not associated with the current federal funds rate decision of the FOMC, but instead with statements that it releases—accounted for more than three-fourths of the explainable variation in the movements of five- and ten-year Treasury yields around FOMC meetings.[7]

The question for the day is, given the importance of words and their impact on market, what can a trader without high-powered economic and computer models do *now* to use word analysis as a technical analysis tool for detecting sentiment? Do we have to wait for greater progress? The answer is that even at this early stage in text mining, the trader can employ this new form of technical analysis of sentiment by using *word* (or *tag*) *clouds*. Word clouds are part of a class of text mining that scans a document and generates word frequency counts and analyses of word associations. A publicly available method and early example of text mining potential is at www.wordle.net. By inserting text into the program, an arrangement of words represented as a function of their frequency is generated. One can instantly see which words are important.

Figure 12.1 is a word cloud of Federal Reserve chairman Ben Bernanke's speech on January 13, 2009 at the London School of Economics.[8]

Let's compare this word cloud with **Figure 12.2**, done for a key speech given by Jean-Claude Trichet, president of the European Central Bank on April 18, 2009. The speech is entitled "The Global Dimensions of the Crisis."[9]

Figure 12.1 Bernanke Speech Analysis: Word Cloud
Source: www.wordle.net

Figure 12.2 Trichet Speech Analysis: Word Cloud
Source: www.wordle.net

A quick comparison of Ben Bernanke's word cloud with the one generated for Jean-Claude Trichet immediately shows some different emphases. The words *global, imbalances,* and *trade* appear prominently in Jean-Claude Trichet's speech, and are comparatively hard to see in Ben Bernanke's speech. The perception of differences between these two key bankers is important to understand, and these word clouds help an investor understand that expectations and sentiment in Europe differ from those in the United States. Word clouds are a step in the right direction, but much more quantification is necessary for text mining to apply to trading. Traders need to know much more than what they can get from word clouds. They need to be alerted to changes in word frequency and emphasis, as well as the detection of new words (new event detection), and whether words are disappearing.

The next steps in technical analysis use of text mining will be to enable any trader to upload a speech or document and a text mining application will generate a word matrix which is an array of words organized so that it shows frequency and compares the change in frequency from one document to another. The application of such a tool will help one gain a better understanding of macro-environment. If we detect a shift in emphasis, it can provide clues about the direction of public policy. What events are being feared? Is it deflation? Inflation? Credit tightening? Asset bubbles? A slight change in emphasis can reveal more to the trader about direction than looking at a chart.

Let's look at the potential demonstrated even at this early level of development. We will do some text mining of Ben Bernanke and Jean-Claude Trichet's speeches and review the results.

There are two types of text mining. The first kind of analysis is similar to a time series. It compares one person's words to previous speeches of the same person. Comparing Ben Bernanke to Jean-Claude Trichet or other persons is an example of *cross-sectional* analysis.

Several dimensions will be of interest to the trader. First is the frequency of key words. Did the use of a word increase or decrease between speeches? Another dimension is the uniqueness of a word's appearance. If a word appears for the first time, it will generate an important signal. When a key policy maker drafts a speech, each word is carefully weighed. The appearance, therefore, of a new word, and its appearance in association with other words (known as *key words in context*) in an economic release or speech can be useful indicators. When comparing one person's words with those of another, the analysis is similar to that of cross-sectional data. Between, for example, Ben Bernanke and Jean-Claude Trichet, some words are common, and some are unique to

Word	Base Speech	Next Speech	Increasing
Federal	8	32	24
Financial	26	46	20
Reserve	5	25	20
Markets	14	32	18
Firms	0	17	17
Funds	1	17	16
Treasury	1	17	16
Assets	1	15	14
Banks	1	15	14
Funding	2	14	12
Economic	8	17	9
Congress	0	8	8
Provide	0	8	8
AIG	0	7	7
Economy	3	10	7
Institutions	7	14	7
Money	0	7	7
Rate	0	7	7
Case	0	6	6
Company	0	6	6
Interest	3	9	6
Liquidity	4	10	6
Program	0	6	6
Should	1	7	6
About	2	7	5
Address	1	6	5
Allow	0	5	5
Authority	0	5	5
Creditors	0	5	5
Legislation	0	5	5
More	7	12	5
Paper	1	6	5

Figure 12.3 Text Mining of Bernanke Speeches: Words of Increasing Frequency

each. There are also variations in the frequency of those words. Let's look at the Sentiment Matrix in action on recent speeches of Bernanke (**Figures 12.3** through **12.5**) and Trichet (**Figure 12.6**). We will first assess Ben Bernanke's speeches in comparison with each other; then we will assess Jean-Claude Trichet's speeches; finally, we will look at Bernanke's speeches in comparison with Trichet's.

Words are both coincident and leading indicators of sentiment. Consider that any official statement by a key government official is carefully scrutinized for the impact every word will have. It therefore makes sense to focus on word appearances, their frequency, and their proximity to other words. An initial scan of a speech breaks down all the words into frequency counts. Frequency counting is the first clue to a shift in sentiment between two speeches. First, we look at which words are increasing in frequency. In comparing two Bernanke speeches, we find a hierarchy of words that significantly increased from the first speech to the second speech (**Figure 12.3**). The increase in frequency is not a coincidence, and provides a direct measure of attitudes. In contrast to prices, which really are results of attitudes, word analysis is a leading indicator. Why does the word *economy* appear three times in Speech 1 and ten times in Speech 2? It is not a coincidence. Why does *creditors* appear zero times in speech 1 but five times in speech 2? The word *balances* appears 0 times in speech 1 but four times in speech 2. The word *liquidity* appears four times in speech 1, but ten times in speech 2.

Decreasing Frequency Comparison

Comparing the same Ben Bernanke speeches with one another, we see a hierarchy of words that have decreased in frequency. For example, in the first speech, the word *prices* appears twenty-one times, and in the second speech, it appears ten times. The word *boom* appears nine times in the first speech and zero times in the second speech. *Inflation* appears ten times in the first speech and five times in the second speech. *Oil* appears six times in the first speech and two times in the second speech. We can see a decreasing emphasis on economic growth, inflation, and boom-related activity by the second speech.

Word	Base Speech	Next Speech	Decreasing
Prices	21	10	–11
Boom	9	0	–9
Domestic	8	0	–8
Longer term	8	0	–8
Subprime	8	0	–8
Global	9	2	–7
Some	12	5	–7
Demand	7	1	–6
Factors	6	0	–6
House	6	0	-6
Rates	6	0	–6
Broader	7	2	–5
High	5	0	–5
Housing	10	5	–5
Inflation	10	5	–5
Rapid	5	0	–5
Risk	7	2	–5
Affected	4	0	–4
Both	9	5	–4
Commodity	5	1	–4
Emerging	5	1	–4
Exchange	4	0	–4
Growth	12	8	–4
Oil	6	2	–4

Figure 12.4 Bernanke Speeches: Decreasing Frequency Analysis

Comparison of Ben Bernanke's and Jean-Claude Trichet's Speeches: A Cross-Sectional Analysis

The trader who wants to get an edge on evaluating macro developments between countries, or even between companies, is currently dependent on lagging macroeconomic indicators and surveys of business attitudes. In the near future, the trader will be able, using text mining, to compare and contrast the word appearances between two different documents. For example, a comparison of the minutes of the central bank of England with the minutes of the Federal Reserve could lead to insights into whether there are significant differences in policy and emphasis. The speeches and annual reports of industry leaders can be mined for data that can be converted into leading indicators about their sectors. In a cross-sectional comparison between two different individual speeches or documents of two different countries, what is important is detecting words that are shared and words that are unique. Let's take a look at two different speeches by Ben Bernanke and Jean-Claude Trichet.

The most frequently mentioned words of Ben Bernanke (**Figure 12.5**), versus those of Jean-Claude Trichet (**Figure 12.6**), in two speeches made not far apart in time, show a clear difference in focus.

When Trichet's remarks were text mined, certain words that are specific or unique to Trichet in comparison with Bernanke were of great interest. Trichet uses the word *refinancing* seventeen times and the word *turbulence* thirteen times. Bernanke uses neither of these words. Notice that Trichet uses the unique word *longer-term,* showing a priority to long-term policy goals. Bernanke doesn't use this word.

Words Shared between Ben Bernanke and Jean-Claude Trichet

We can also examine words shared by Ben Bernanke and Jean-Claude Trichet. In these words, a frequency difference is very revealing. Bernanke mentions the word *credit* twenty-three times, while Trichet mentions it three times. Bernanke mentions the word *economy* eleven times, and Trichet mentions it once. Ben Bernanke mentions the word *financial* twenty-eight times, and Jean-Claude Trichet uses it fourteen times. Most revealing is that Bernanke refers to *markets* sixteen times, compared with Trichet's four.

Text Mining of Federal Open Market Committee Statements

The entire trading world waits to see what the Federal Open Market Committee (FOMC) will say when it releases its statements. These

Word	Bernanke Specific
Subprime	24
Federal	17
Mortgages	15
Discount	14
Prices	14
Housing	13
Window	13
Growth	12
Inflation	11
Investors	11
Borrowers	9
Products	9
Broader	7
Institutions	7
Securities	7
Tax	7
Vehicles	7
Funds	6
Further	6
Investment	6
Mortgage	6
Notably	6
Risks	6
Strains	6
Structured	6

Figure 12.5 Text Mining of Bernanke-Specific Words

statements are not lengthy; they number approximately sixty-five words. Therefore, every word is considered very carefully. It is common wisdom that these statements move the market in the moments after their release.

Word	Trichet Specific
Refinancing	17
Euro	13
Turbulence	13
Area	12
Eurosystem	12
Eurosystem's	9
Provided	9
Ecb	8
Framework	8
European	7
Longerterm	6
Maintenance	6
Observed	6
Operational	6
Tensions	6
Allowed	5
Cooperation	4
Exceptional	4
Main	4
Maturity	4
October	4
Procedures	4
Three	4
Agreement	3
Alleviate	3
Allotment	3

Figure 12.6 Text Mining of Trichet-Specific Words

On January 22, 2008, an extraordinary statement was issued when the FOMC cut interest rates by 75 basis points. Only eight days later, it cut rates by another 50 basis points. These statements moved the markets. A side-by-side analysis where one can read each statement and contrast the statements' emphasis on key words is a common method used today.

This method is very cumbersome. With text mining, it can be nearly instant. When the statements in **Table 12.1** are text mined for frequency of words and for unique word occurrence, tracking each key word over a period of time, we can obtain a deeper understanding of nuances and shifts in sentiment. This frequency charting is a new type of charting that will be available to the trader soon. We text mined every FOMC statement from January 31,

Table 12.1 Side-by-side display of Federal Open Market Committee Statements published by Bloomberg L.P.

January 30, 2008 Text	January 22 Text
The Federal Open Market Committee decided today to lower its target for the federal funds rate 50 basis points to 3 percent.	The Federal Open Market Committee has decided to lower its target for the federal funds rate 75 basis points to 3-1/2 percent.
Financial markets remain under considerable stress, and credit has tightened further for some businesses and households. Moreover, recent information indicates a deepening of the housing contraction as well as some softening in labor markets.	The Committee took this action in view of a weakening of the economic outlook and increasing downside risks to growth. While strains in short-term funding markets have eased somewhat, broader financial market conditions have continued to deteriorate and credit has tightened further for some businesses and households. Moreover, incoming information indicates a deepening of the housing contraction as well as some softening in labor markets.
The Committee expects inflation to moderate in coming quarters, but it will be necessary to continue to monitor inflation developments carefully.	The Committee expects inflation to moderate in coming quarters, but it will be necessary to continue to monitor inflation developments carefully.
Today's policy action, combined with those taken earlier, should help to promote moderate growth over time and to mitigate the risks to economic activity. However, downside risks to growth remain. The Committee will continue to assess the effects of financial and other developments on economic prospects and will act in a timely manner as needed to address those risks.	Appreciable downside risks to growth remain. The Committee will continue to assess the effects of financial and other developments on economic prospects and will act in a timely manner as needed to address those risks.

2007 to April 30, 2009. The text-mining software we used is found at http://www.sobolsoft.com.

We selected several key words and tracked them starting with the January 2007 statements. We can see the word *economic* rise in frequency (**Figure 12.7**), reflecting a growing economic concern. In contrast, the word *inflation* (**Figure 12.8**) has had several swings in emphasis and has substantially declined in usage. Of course, the word *federal*, hardly used at all for years, took a sudden spike in the later months (**Figure 12.9**). The word *market* has also a variation in emphasis over time (**Figure 12.10**). The usage of the word *growth* (**Figure 12.11**) is interesting because of its precipitous decline after peak use in August 2008.

Key questions arise. Which words are increasing in emphasis? Which words are decreasing? The proposition here is that charting words in their appearances over time is an important emerging form of technical and sentiment analysis.

FOMC Minutes

The minutes of central bank meetings are also released, and have an impact on the market. Text mining of the minutes enables the trader to detect variations in sentiment. Programs now offer visualization of the importance that words have in a document. These can use color and shapes to show variations in significance. The color red, for example, commonly highlights important words. Eagle Software in France processed text files of FOMC minutes for December 16, 2008, January 28, 2009, and March 18, 2009 for us, and developed a representation method that organizes key words and represents them in cells. (The full table breaking down the words is in **Figure 12.12**) The graphic for each date (**Figures 12.13** through **12.15**) indicates these words' importance through color, size of cell, and distance from center.

The top twenty-five words provide a virtual inventory of the concepts tracked by policymakers. From a trader's perspective, the differences among the sets of minutes are the important thing to focus on. Here is one key example: the word *decline* had 17 percent frequency on December 16. That frequency went to 10 percent on March 18. Meanwhile, the word *inflation* stayed within a 5–7 percent range.

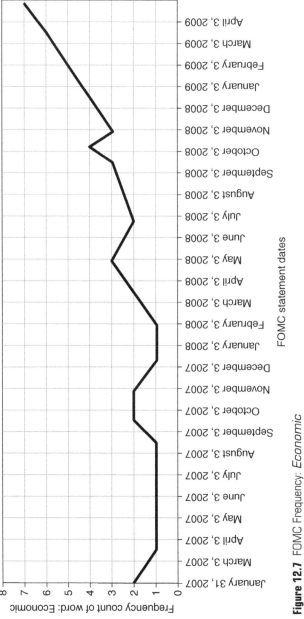

Figure 12.7 FOMC Frequency: *Economic*

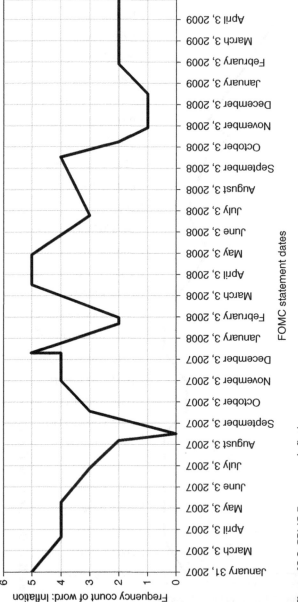

Figure 12.8 FOMC Frequency: *Inflation*

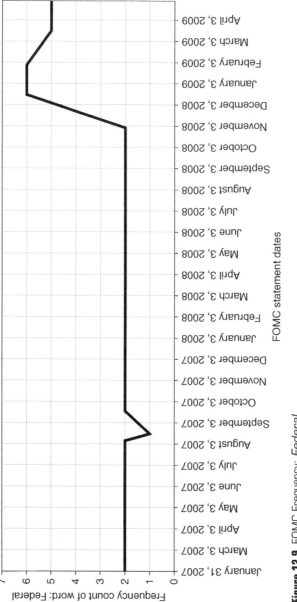

Figure 12.9 FOMC Frequency: *Federal*

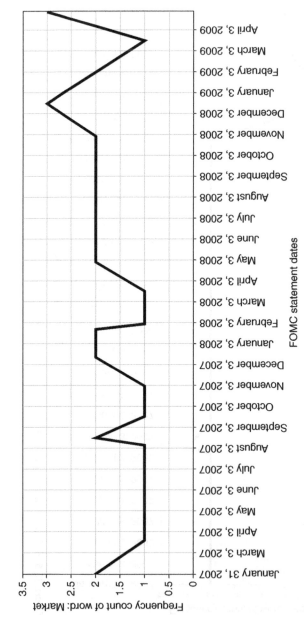

Figure 12.10 FOMC Frequency: *Market*

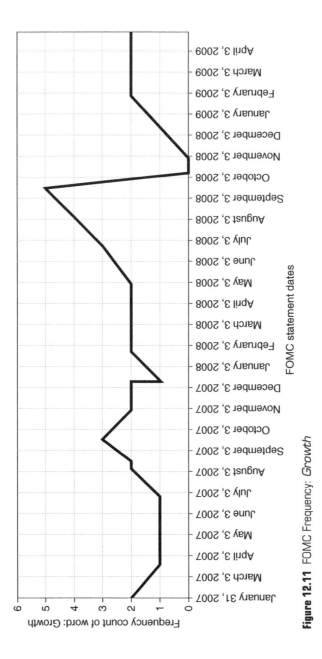

Figure 12.11 FOMC Frequency: *Growth*

	A	B	C	D	E	F	G	H	I	J	K
1	**Minutes for December 16**				**Minutes for January 28**				**Minutes for March 18**		
2	Key Word	Presence of word in # of texts	Percentage		Key Word	Presence of word in # of texts	Percentage		Key Word	Presence of word in # of texts	Percentage
3	market	76	21%		Market	97	17%		federal	43	13%
4	decline	60	17%		federal	78	13%		reserve	38	11%
5	federal	54	15%		reserve	64	11%		purchase	36	11%
6	price	49	14%		bank	63	11%		decline	34	10%
7	economic	45	12%		foreign	53	9%		bank	32	10%
8	rate	45	12%		decline	47	8%		financial	32	10%
9	condition	42	12%		system	45	8%		February	31	9%
10	reserve	42	12%		currency	43	7%		rate	31	9%
11	activity	39	11%		condition	40	7%		price	30	9%
12	participant	39	11%		economic	40	7%		continue	28	8%
13	continue	36	10%		price	40	7%		economic	27	8%
14	financial	31	9%		financial	39	7%		condition	26	8%
15	further	31	9%		credit	38	7%		increase	26	8%
16	remain	30	8%		open	38	7%		Treasury	25	8%
17	Fund	29	8%		Security	38	7%		securities	24	7%
18	monetary	28	8%		period	32	6%		further	22	7%
19	credit	26	7%		rate	31	5%		program	21	6%
20	policy	26	7%		meet	31	5%		remain	21	6%
21	October	25	7%		Treasury	31	5%		level	20	6%
22	quarter	25	7%		increase	29	5%		quarter	20	6%
23	inflation	24	7%		program	29	5%		credit	19	6%
24	bank	23	6%		operation	29	5%		business	17	5%
25	increase	23	6%		purchase	27	5%		debt	16	5%

Figure 12.12 Summary of Key Words Across All Dates

Source: eeagle.com

246

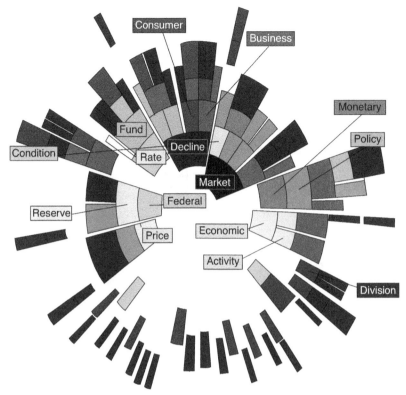

Figure 12.13 Key Word Visualization, FOMC Minutes, December 16, 2007
Source: eeagle.com

Comparing Trichet Testimony with Bernanke Testimony

On January 10, 2008, Ben Bernanke delivered an important speech on the financial markets. One year and one month later, on February 20, 2009, Jean-Claude Trichet gave a speech about the ECB's response to the financial crises. Using text-mining analysis, we can detect words that were coincident and words that were unique to each policy maker. What is striking about the comparison is the words unique to each speaker. They show that, although the financial crisis was a global one, the mindset of these policy makers led to important differences in what they emphasized. Trichet's most frequent twenty words reveal that he is clearly Eurocentric in outlook, focusing on responses to the crisis as a process, whereas Bernanke

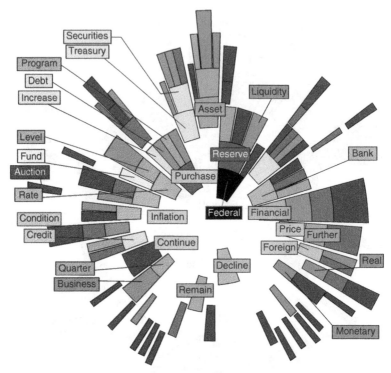

Figure 12.14 Key Word Visualization, FOMC Minutes, January 28, 2008
Source: eeagle.com

was at that time focused on the housing market–related causes of the crises.[10]

One can see how words can become leading indicators of market expectations. The future of sentiment analysis will be in the direction of extracting real-time information from key statements of policy makers. Real-time word charts showing word frequency, co-occurrences of words, and differences among statements by key policy makers will soon become an everyday tool for the trader. What is important and exciting to realize is that when text mining enables real-time word analysis, words themselves will become units of sentiment and a new class of indicators and signals will arise. That time is not far away.

Text mining as a part of technical analysis of price action is here to stay.

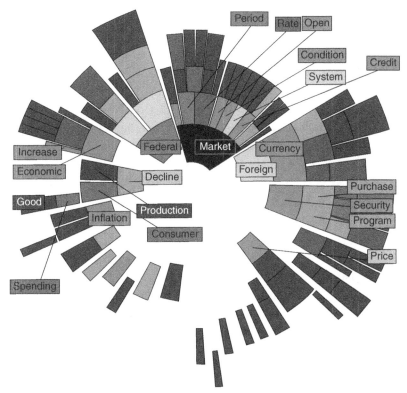

Figure 12.15 Key Word Visualization, FOMC Minutes, March 18, 2009
Source: eeagle.com

Chapter Notes

1. Subhash R. Lele and Joan T. Richtsmeier, *An Invariant Approach to Statistical Analysis of Shapes*. Boca Raton, FL: Chapman & Hall, 2001.

2. http://palstrat.unigraz.at/methods%20in%20ostracodology/Contr GeomMorphom_vol13Berr(080708).

3. Nii Ayi Armah and Norman R. Swanson, "Seeing Inside the Black Box: Using Diffusion Index Methodology to Construct Factor Proxies in Large Scale Macroeconomic Time Series Environments." Federal Reserve Bank of Philadelphia Working Paper 08–19, July 2008, retrieved from http://www.philadelphiafed.org/research-and-data/publications/working-papers/2008/wp08-19.pdf.

4. Ibid.

5. Uta Hellinger, Event and Sentiment Detection in Financial Markets, AIFB, Universität Karlsruhe, Germany, hellinger@aifb.uni-karlsruhe.de.

6. G. Pui Cheong Fung, J. Xu Yu, and Wai Lam, Stock Prediction: Integrating Text Mining Approach Using Real-Time News. In Proceedings, IEEE International Conference on Computational Intelligence for Financial Engineering, Hong Kong, 2003, 395–402.

7. Refet S., Gurkaynak, Brian P. Sack, and Eric T., Swanson, Do Actions Speak Louder Than Words? The Response of Asset Prices to Monetary Policy Actions and Statements (November 2004). FEDS Working Paper No. 2004-66. Available at SSRN: http://ssrn.com/abstract=633281 86.

8. http://www.federalreserve.gov/newsevents/speech/bernanke20080110a.htm

9. http://www.ecb.int/press/key/date/2009/html/sp090418.en.html.

10. http://www.ecb.int/press/key/date/2009/html/sp090220.en.html; http://www.federalreserve.gov/newsevents/speech/bernanke20080110a.htm.

CHAPTER 13

Beyond the Trend
Cycle Indicators
Independent of Time

THE AIM OF this chapter is to present in more detail how the cycle indicator can become an important addition to technical analysis.

A goal of this book has been to advance the ability of traders to detect price patterns and discern when they change. The conventional method has been to use charts that filter out time in looking at price movement, and to detect changes in the trend condition of a price. We certainly know now that price break, Kagi, Renko, and point and figure charting help clarify detection of changes in price patterns from different vantage points. These charts create boundaries or landmarks that verify changes in the price direction or pattern. But are they enough? How can the trader uncover even more about the price behavior that is being evaluated?

Luckily, the quest for knowledge that can give the trader an edge doesn't stop with candlestick, price break, Kagi, Renko, or point and figure. There is a new generation of advanced technical indicators that can also enable the trader to detect hidden patterns in price data. Some of these indicators come from physics, and others come from the field of manufacturing control. Few traders have heard of them because they are used as research tools, and only now are coming into the hands of the trader through retail software products. Traders should seriously consider them, because when used alone or with alternative charts, these indicators provide new insights for the trader. The overall function of these new forms of indicators is to filter out the noise and pinpoint the regularity of a pattern. These indicators apply known advances in statistical analysis and science. They are known collectively as *cycle indicators.* Let's look at some examples and their applications to trading analysis.

Cycle Detection and Projection

Beyond recognizing the obvious fact that price patterns very often seem to reoccur, the enormous challenge is to find out what the underlying pattern is. Even if a price is visually recognized to be in a trend or in a sideways pattern, the data that generated the chart is unprocessed raw data. The scientific fact is that it may also have within it a wave. We have already introduced the idea that a channel pattern is really a form of a wave. However, especially when one uses high-frequency data and small time intervals, the presence of waves is not easy to detect. The average trader does not have the tools, beyond simple visual analysis, to decipher the cycles in the patterns, and as a result, he ignores them. The consequence is that he misses important alerts about price direction and possible turning points. None of the alternative charting tools we have discussed can detect waves in the prices. They all work on visualizing the raw price data. The important question that a trader should try to answer is whether the observed changes in the prices coincide with wave-like embedded turning points. For example, in **Figure 13.1a**, we see a pattern that looks very much like a price chart. Any trader would identify areas in this chart as trend lines. A closer look reveals that this chart is just a pattern generated by the following equation using Mathematica software (**Figure13.1b**).

The point is that a trader needs to unmask the hidden patterns that generate the chart.

Next time you look at a chart, remember that it is likely that a hidden pattern generated the price patterns. While it is human nature to think of price movements as linear, they do not have to be. In fact, a great many of the patterns behind the prices are cyclical waveforms. Ignoring this real possibility leads to misinterpreting the path that prices are likely to take.

What is a Wave?

Let's first review exactly what a wave is. Most readers have forgotten basic geometry and trigonometry, but the world has known about waves

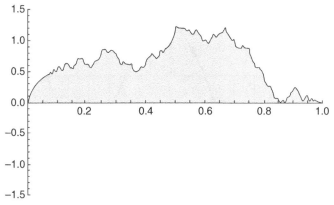

Figure 13.1a Simulated Price Action from Mathematical Equation
Source: Mathematica.com

$$\sum_{k=1}^{\infty} \frac{\alpha\cos(k^\beta\pi x) + (1-\alpha)\sin(k^\beta\pi x)}{k^\beta}$$

Figure 13.1b Mathematical Equation
Source: Mathematica.com

for thousands of years. Mathematical historians cite the discovery of the geometry of waves as dating back to 200 BC, during the time of Hipparchus.

A wave is a function that is mathematically composed of a sine wave. The wavy form in **Figure 13.2** should be very familiar.

One of the most confirmed cycles in nature is the eleven-year sunspot cycle. Its peaks and troughs **(Figure 13.3)** are highly predictable.

Another example of a wave, this time formed by a combination of two tones, is shown in **Figure 13.4**.

Both the sunspot cycle and the two-tone cycle are natural, real cycles and are indisputably part of the physics of their phenomena.

So what about price data? Is it cyclical? Let's look at some real data. We used one-minute data of the AUDUSD. Statistical analysis of this data indicated that there was a significant wave at a sixteen-minute interval. We were able to transform the one-minute data into five different types of waves: rectified sine, sawtooth, regular sine, square, and triangle **(Figures 13.5–13.9)**.

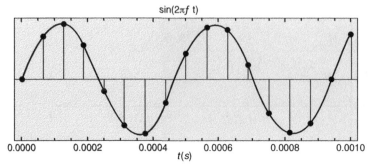

Figure 13.2 Common Sine Wave

Source: Mathematica.com

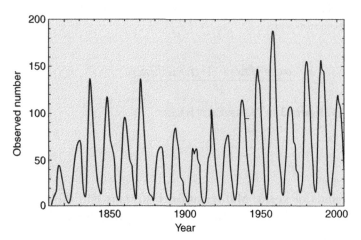

Figure 13.3 Eleven-Year Sunspot Cycle

Source: Mathematica.com

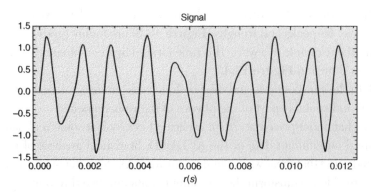

Figure 13.4 Two-Tone Cycle

Source: Mathematica.com

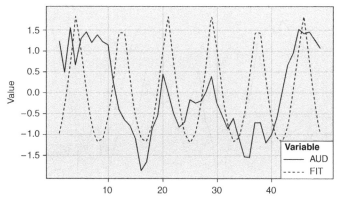

Figure 13.5 One-Minute AUDUSD: Rectified Sine Wave
Source: Abe Cofnas and Joseph Egbulefu

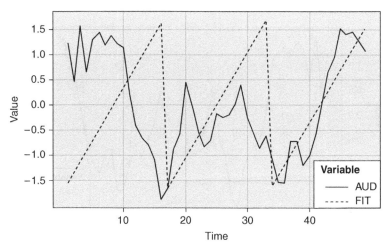

Figure 13.6 One-Minute AUDUSD: Sawtooth Wave
Source: Abe Cofnas and Joseph Egbulefu

The next task is to decide which one is the best fit. Notice that in all the different wave types, there are instances where the turning points of the waves coincide with the data peaks and troughs.

The trader needs to be sensitive to exactly what is being presented when cycles are displayed. A sine wave appears more frequently. Additionally, a composite of waves is commonly presented. **Figure 13.10** shows an integration of the four waves of the one-minute AUD.

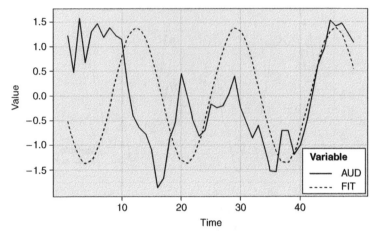

Figure 13.7 One-Minute AUDUSD: Sine Wave

Source: Abe Cofnas and Joseph Egbulefu

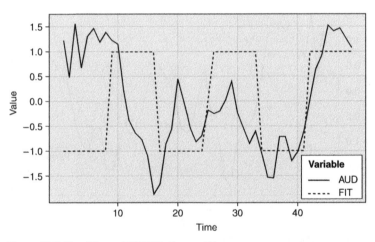

Figure 13.8 One-Minute AUDUSD: Square Wave

Source: Abe Cofnas and Joseph Egbulefu

The challenge, when using cycle indicators, is to make sure that the wave form that is represented clearly indicates it is a composite wave form representing an attempt to generate the best fit.

The main idea behind cycle indicators is to flush out what kinds of waves are embedded in the price data. Why waves appear is not answerable. They are part of the fabric of nature. Whenever energy is

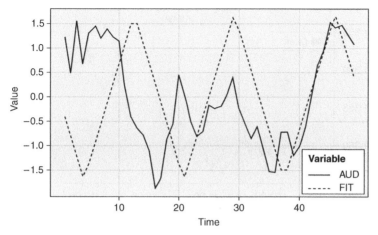

Figure 13.9 One-Minute AUDUSD: Triangle Wave
Source: Abe Cofnas and Joseph Egbulefu

used, waveforms are part of it. It is similar to the question of why Fibonacci ratios work. A wave initiation can be the result of an exogenous event, such as news, that ignites an expansion of price over time, resulting in a peak, and then a contraction, and then a trough. A wave may also be a hidden pattern in the price behavior itself. No one can predict what will cause a wave. Let's just agree that waves are part of the fabric of how nature and energy work, and that they do appear in price action.

While we did not intend this chapter to be a course in wave physics, a few key features of waves are important to understand. These include *amplitude, period,* and *frequency.*

➤ Amplitude = Height of wave
➤ Period = Time it takes to complete one wave
➤ Frequency = Number of oscillations per period (1/Period)

If we detect a wave cycle in the price data, it will have all of these features. If the indicator is valid, it will detect the origin and project the cycle into the future. Such a projection also forecasts the peaks and troughs. In effect, it becomes a timing device and a confirming indicator of other tools of technical analysis. Notice that the emphasis is on confirmation and not on isolated use of wave cycle indicators.

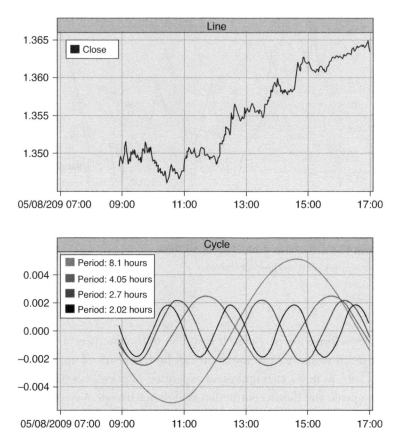

Figure 13.10 Composite Wave
Source: Abe Cofnas and Joseph Egbulefu

The task for technical analysis is therefore to enable traders to generate the best-fitting waves for any series of data. This is not a trivial task, and it is critical to understanding how to view price action. The trader views the actual price, but can't detect hidden patterns. Cycle-based indicators break down the price or "time series" into different components. When the price data is de-trended and unmasked, the trader will see a familiar trend component represented by a straight line. Cycle programs that do not de-trend the data are not following accepted practice of statistics.

There is also a seasonal component of periodic swings that can be the result of outside but predictable conditions. After going through some advanced statistical processing (which with today's computers is very easy to program), we arrive at the cyclical components of the price data. If the data has a periodic peak and trough, and goes through contractions and expansions, a cycle has been discovered.

The last component of any series of data is a random component: the noise. Noise cannot be explained and is nonrepeating and irregular.

Put all these components back together and you get the traditional chart. This has astounding implications: To understand the patterns behind the chart will require deconstructing the chart into the various elements we have discussed. Let's review how this kind of deconstruction occurs in current practice.

Methodology for Generating Cycle Waves

Fourier Analysis

The current generation of cycle indicators uses *Fourier analysis*, which is a standard method of filtering noise out of price data. The term *harmonic analysis,* which has appeared in technical analysis literature, actually relates to the Fourier technique. What Fourier analysis does is take data and construct wave patterns around the data. There are several ways for a trader to generate a Fourier-type analysis. A well-informed trader with Excel can generate Fourier waves using available standard equations.

Using one-minute AUDUSD data **(Figure 13.11)**, we can see where the prices peaked in coincidence with peaks in the cycle, and where bottoms occurred in coincidence with troughs.

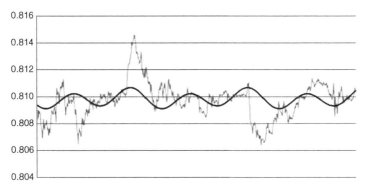

Figure 13.11 Fourier Analysis of AUD One-Minute Price Data

Source: Abe Cofnas and Joseph Egbulefu

A key next step is to project or forecast the cycle wave into the near future. Cycle users need to keep in mind that the longer the forecast period the greater the potential for an error in the forecast. **Figure 13.12** shows how it looks.

There is no doubt that cycles exist in price action and can be detected and visualized. Advances have made cycle analysis and tools available at a retail level to the trader. Here are some key questions to ask before you purchase a cycle indicator package:

What is the methodology generating the cycle? Essentially, cycle methodology is based on Fourier analysis and its variations. These include standard Fourier and fast Fourier.

How many data points are needed to generate the cycle wave? Some vendors require more data points than do others. Beware of the vendors that require a relatively small set of data points. Cycle detection, to be reliable, requires more data points, not fewer.

Does the software project a cycle wave into the future? How far? Depending on the time series, projections could extend over many periods into the future. This would allow verification of the forecasting power of the cycle tool.

Can you upload your own data series into the software and generate your own wave? This is an important capability, as it allows the serious trader to evaluate his own data.

Does the software indicate measures of the accuracy of the wave fit? Look to see if there is any data plotting a profit-and-loss scenario using the projected wave. The ability to provide a high-probable fit for a projected turning point is the goal of any software and a criterion for its evaluation.

Cycles and Volume Data

The applications of cycle analysis go beyond price data. Applying cycle analysis to volume data can be very productive for the trader. The conventional wisdom shows that volume is a barometer of sentiment. When you apply a cycle analysis to volume data, you can then use projected peaks or bottoms in volume to help shape trading strategy. In **Figure 13.13**, we see a sine wave generated by volume data.

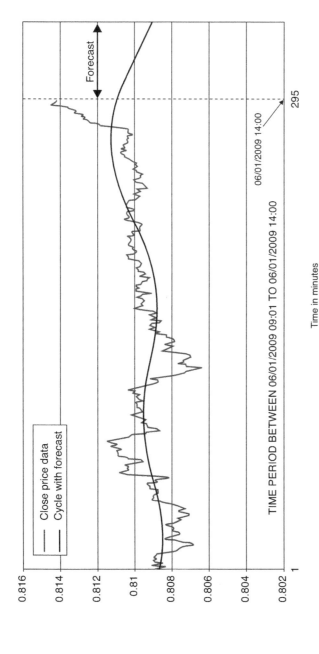

Figure 13.12 AUDUSD 1-Minute Cycle Projection

Source: Abe Cofnas and Joseph Egbulefu

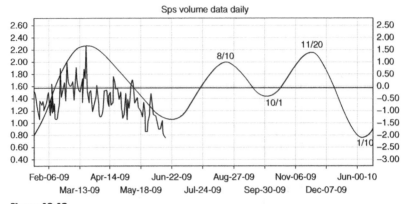

Figure 13.13

Source: Abe Cofnas and Joseph Egbulefu

Wavelet Cycles Are Coming

A new type of cycle detection and projection indicator that goes beyond Fourier analysis is now underway. It promises to be a very significant addition to the trader's toolbox. It is known as wavelets. Wavelets go further than Fourier analysis and the programs that slice the price data into small sections, decompose the data into the key parts of a trend or cycle, and identify turning points. The wavelet then projects out into the near future identifying a probable next path for the prices. It promises to be much more useful than current Fourier analysis. The trader who is serious about using cycle indicators as part of the total toolbox of trading should keep a watch for wavelet applications. **Table 13.1** compares Fourier analysis and wavelets.

Table 13.1 Fourier Analysis and Wavelets Compared

Comparison Metric	Fourier Transform Method	Wavelets
Basis	Sines and cosines.	Basis constructed by shifting and by vertical and horizontal scaling of certain prototype general functions called *wavelets*.
Price data assumption— Signal content	Method assumes that the input price data series is the representation of an infinite sum of sinusoids with a various phase, amplitude, and frequency.	Method is flexible and hence does not place any restrictive assumptions on the data series.

Table 13.1 *(Continued)*

Comparison Metric	Fourier Transform Method	Wavelets
Price data assumption— Frequency content	Method assumes signal *stationarity*, meaning that the frequency content remains unchanged over time and all frequency components in the price data series exist at all times.	Method handles nonstationary signals. This means that the frequency of signal components in the time-series data may change over time. Wavelets can also capture frequency components that appear, disappear, and then reappear over time.
Price data feature capture— trends, abrupt changes, discontinuities	Cannot capture these features due to the sine/cosine basis assumption in the Fourier transformation (FT) process.	Can capture trends, abrupt changes, and discontinuities in the time-series price data because the wavelet transformation basis is flexible.
Process flexibility	Fourier transformation process is inflexible due to its basis and input data stationarity assumptions. Short-Time Fourier Transform (STFT) improves on FT. The time-series data is divided into small segments and the signal on each of these segments is assumed as stationary. Drawbacks of STFT: No inverse process, i.e., original signal cannot be reconstructed; window size chosen is the same for all frequencies—impractical since window sizing needs scaling up for low frequencies and vice versa for high-frequency signals.	Flexible process. Wavelet transform employs windowing techniques with variable-sized regions. This allows handling of high-frequency components for a short duration (bursts) and low-frequency components for long durations (trends). Ability to project prices in the presence of trends, abrupt changes, and discontinuities is essential, and wavelet transforms does not overlook these in the input time series.
Multiscale time-frame analysis	Does poorly on multiscale time-frame analysis.	Allows multiscale analysis of prices on various time frames by separating traders into various groups: scalpers, day traders, swing traders, and position traders.
Applicability as a price forecasting tool	Because of the suppositions placed on the input data, it is a restrictive forecasting tool for time-series price data.	Wavelets can be used effectively with neural networks, genetic algorithms, and other methods to forecast prices.
Performance	Operations, although efficient, are not so efficient when handling massive amount of time-series data.	Operations (is faster). Computationally efficient. Can be used in real time with large masses of tick data.

Source: Abe Cofnas and Sridhar Iyer

Finally, grey wave curve prediction and projections have emerged as the latest variation of projecting cycle waves with financial and price data. Chen Keja and Zhang Qishen at Fuzhou University in Fuzhou, China are pioneering work with economic cycle prediction using the new method of grey wave analysis. These researchers developed a methodology for curve prediction that worked very accurately with Chinese economic survey data.[1]

We can conclude that the next generation of cycle indicators will generate exciting tools for use with all data and chart forms.

Chapter Note

1. Chen Keja and Zhang Qishen, Grey Systems and Intelligent Services. IEEE International Conference on Grey Systems and Intelligent Services. Nanjing, China, November 2007, 693–695.

Epilogue

THIS BOOK HAS explored new ways to increase the power of technical analysis by going beyond candlesticks and applying price break, Kagi, Renko, point and figure, and cycle charts in new ways. It also demonstrates an integrated approach not seen before. These chart types have been in existence for a long time, in many cases for over one hundred years. Now, in combination with new data integration and visualization displays, they can become more powerful tools than ever before. It is somewhat extraordinary that charting concepts that predate computer technology, long abandoned as archaic, can now be resurrected and become more relevant. This is the result of the stages of technological innovation we have witnessed. The first generation of self-directed traders (starting about 1996, with the appearance of the Netscape browser) enjoyed the breakthrough of being able to trade at a desktop computer. This was the start of the online self-directed trading revolution. The second phase of trading started with the arrival of laptop mobility. The third phase of technology is being experienced today with the emergence of low-cost flat screen displays that allow the trader to use multiple screens to enhance the ability to simultaneously scan more charts than ever before. Many traders can now have four or more screens. The next manifestation of digital technology will be homes with trading walls! In fact, "screen" is the wrong term to use. Instead, we should think of these displays as *analytical surfaces*. It is possible to dedicate each screen to the display of a distinct chart type or category of information.

The coming era of trading technology can be termed the era of the "smart" chart and the "smart" platform. The platforms and charts of the near future will not simply execute at near–nano-based speeds, but will also act as embedded coaches, providing information from several time frames and several markets at the same time. There is no reason that price break, Kagi, point and figure, and Renko charts can't be embedded with information that represents other technical conditions of the price action. For example, the price break chart of the near future will be able to have a price break that occurs at a 61.8 percent Fibonacci line change colors to signify this event. The Kagi chart of the near future, when generating a shift from a Yin to a Yang or a Yang to a Yin, will be able to flash if it is near a three-price break reversal point or a key Fibonacci line. Almost any condition that we can derive from price data can infuse these charts with more information. We have also explored how new indicators using cycle detection can provide yet additional methods for evaluating if the price action is changing its pattern, breaking its trend, or resuming a prior pattern.

The applications in this book provide in-depth and innovative approaches for the use of alternative charts.

The technical analysis of mapping sentiment data does not stop here. We have also explored the emergence of text mining as a form of real-time sentiment analysis. Words, if tracked correctly, provide insights into broad sentiment changes and policy nuances that can help the trader separate the noise from the information.

Technical analysis can no longer be myopic and needs to reflect all of the dimensions and forces that create sentiment. By applying alternative charting, text mining, and cycle analysis, a more complete approach to understanding price action is achievable.

Index

About the Author

Abe Cofnas is a leading forex trainer and analyst. Since 2001, he has been *Futures* magazine's forex trader columnist, writing over 100 columns and providing strategies and tactics on mastering forex trading. He has conducted seminars throughout the United States and in London and Dubai on fundamental and technical analysis tools for understanding currency for the Online Trading Academy and related markets. In 2001, Mr. Cofnas founded www.learn4x.com to provide online training on forex trading, including innovative techniques in the use of price break and Renko charting. Cofnas recently formed www.fxdimensions.com, a company that develops behavioral finance algorithms that generate trader performance analytics and apply risk and leverage controls for trading teams. He was a technical analyst consultant to Weiss Research Inc., has served as an equity broker, and traded both futures and forex markets. Cofnas holds two master's degrees (in political science and public policy) from the University of California at Berkeley. He is the author of *The Forex Trading Course* and *The Forex Options Trading Course*. He resides in Orlando, Florida.

Printed and bound by CPI Group (UK) Ltd, Croydon, CR0 4YY

16/04/2025

14658510-0002